Excel Easy Vol. 1

Financial Management Dashboard

A quick step-by-step guide to get inspired and create an easy dashboard
using Microsoft Excel

Create and Learn

createandlearn.net

contact.createandlearn@gmail.com

createandlearn.net

https://www.linkedin.com/company/create-and-learn/

ISBN: 9798647838711

1.Contents

For more **Excel Easy** books, visit createandlearn.net/exceleasy

Step into the Business Intelligence and Data Science World!

Visit createandlearn.net

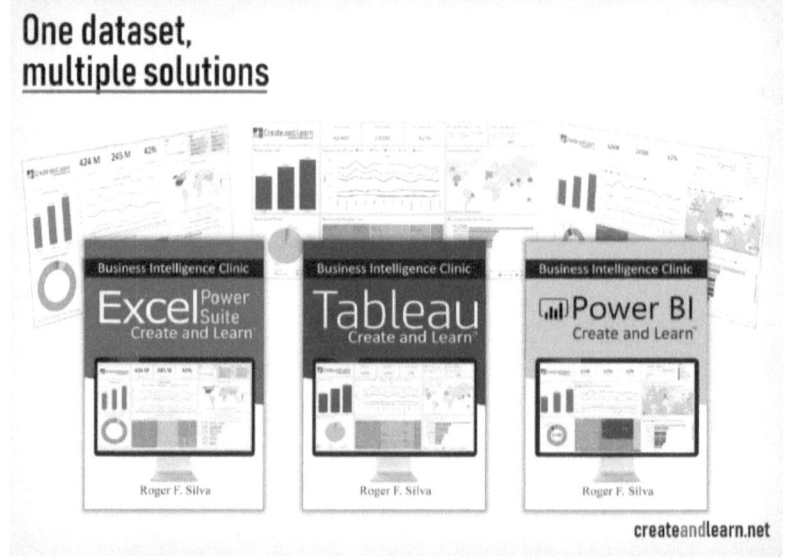

2.Introduction

Dear Reader,

The **Excel Easy** is a series of short books that help students and professionals improve their ability to create beautiful and professional deliverables, using Microsoft Excel, through easy and quick step-by-step instructions.

With this series, you will have the opportunity to work with datasets, metrics, and Key Performance Indicators (KPIs) from a wide range of industries, helping you become a valuable resource to any team and business.

In this book, **Excel Easy Vol 1 – Financial Management Dashboard**, which has over 100 images, you will create a unique Dashboard for finance using basic and intermediate customization tools and Dashboard Design methods.

Our promises: Few pages, quick steps, and professional deliverables.

This volume is for beginners and people who want to get inspired by creating beautiful dashboards. We will not go into deep theories as to the purpose of this book, and all Create and Learn material is to make the most of your time and learn by doing.

We hope this book will help start your journey in the Business Intelligence world and provide the necessary tools to create professional reports and dashboards using Microsoft Excel.

You can find more books and information on the website createandlearn.net/exceleasy

Thank you for creating and learning.

Create and Learn Team

contact.createandlearn@gmail.com

createandlearn.net

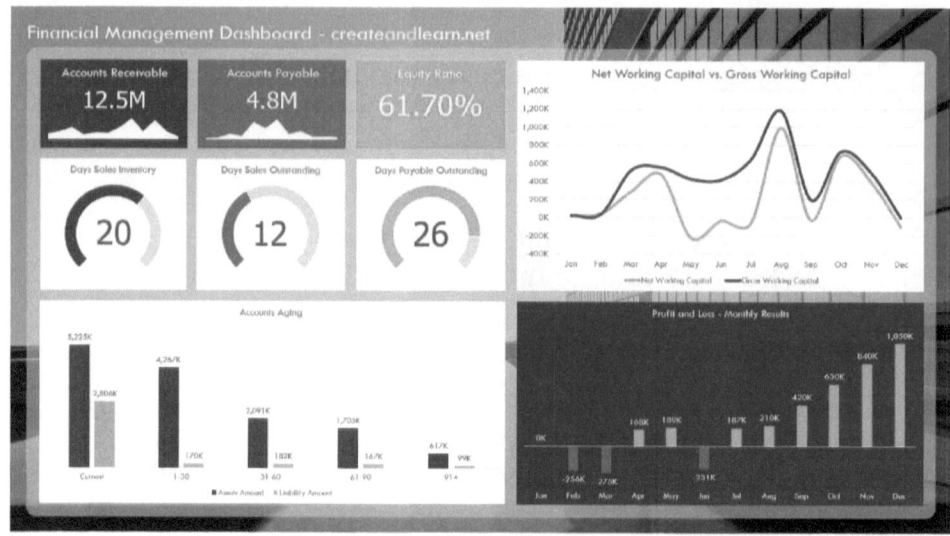

Dashboard to be created in this book

Challenge proposed

3.Data Dashboard

In simple terms, a data dashboard is an information management tool that will track, analyze, and visually display metrics, critical data points, and Key Performance Indicators (KPIs). This allows users to monitor how well a business, department, or specific process is performing.

A data dashboard can be tailored to the specific needs of any company or department. What this tool does is essentially take your attachments, files, APIs, and services, and display all the inline data charts, bar charts, tables, and gauges so you can have a complete perspective of your business, department, or specific process.

If you are looking for an efficient way to keep track of various data sources, a data dashboard is what you need. It will provide a central location where you can monitor and analyze performance in an organized, real-time manner. This will cut back the time spent analyzing information, and it will improve communication and decision-making.

To further understand how a data dashboard can benefit you and your business, let's take a look at how it works and what you can do to create it.

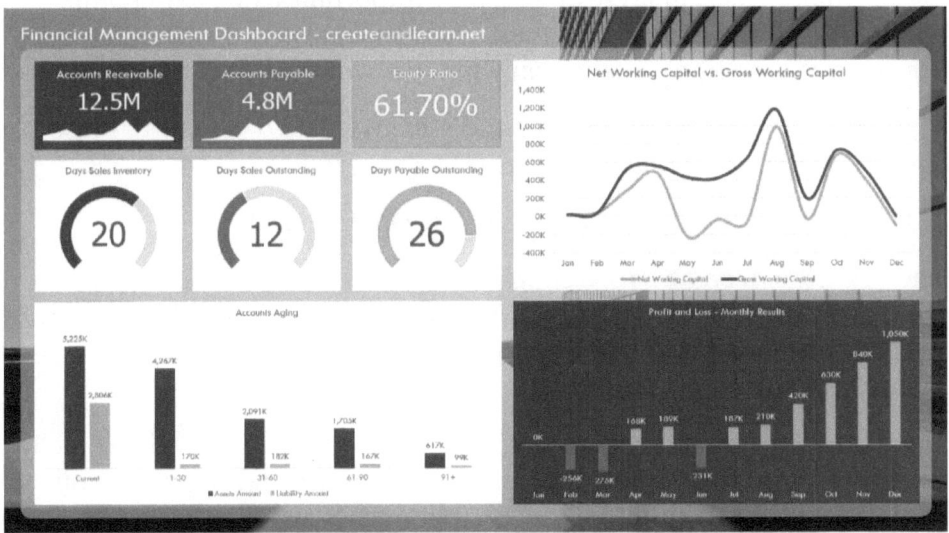

Data Dashboards: How Do They Work?

The beauty of data dashboards is they are highly customizable. They can be tailored to whatever role you need them to play. This means the way they work will depend entirely on how they are being used. Not all data dashboards will be used for the same purposes; that is why it's crucial to determine the KPIs you want to track and why you want to track them.

The best data dashboards will answer the most critical questions about your business. They are designed for quick analysis and to increase information awareness, after all, so they need to answer relevant questions. For this reason, one of the most common approaches to designing a data dashboard is the question-answer format.

What questions the data dashboard is meant to answer will depend entirely on the industry of your business, the process, department, or position you are looking into, etc. These questions will be answered based on insights from the data collected, and they are meant to guide decision-makers and leaders to understand why something happened the way it did, set goals, and more.

How to Make an Effective Data Dashboard

As mentioned before, a data dashboard is all about communication. It allows you to track, analyze and display important KPIs, data points and metrics from multiple sources. This means you can customize it however you see fit depending on what you want to do with it.

If you want to create a successful and effective data dashboard, these 10 tips will help you do that effortlessly!

1. Determine the Focus of the Data Dashboard

The first step in creating a compelling data dashboard is determining what problem you want to solve. Your data dashboard must have a clear purpose; if there is no need for it, you'll only be wasting time and resources on it.

Once you determine the focus of the data dashboard, you will be able to identify the metrics you need to analyze, measure, and improve. You should have 5 to 10 essential metrics per dashboard. This will provide a clear understanding of the value you are adding (or not), which will help you paint a clear picture to stakeholders.

2. Know Who Will Look at the Data Dashboard

When you are creating a data dashboard, you must tailor it to the people who will be looking at it. Knowing the audience will help you make sure you are creating the right board for them so they can make the most of it.

The first thing you need to determine is what problems will the data dashboard be solving. The data dashboard needs to be aligned with the needs of the user. Once you have determined that, you will need to choose the right metrics for the people who will be using the data dashboard. It is also essential to understand what these people will gain from the data dashboard; what are their goals?

Once you know all this, you will be able to create a data dashboard that will perfectly suit the audience. If you are creating it for yourself, it's essential to determine all these factors before you get to work.

3. Organize the Content from Left to Right

How you organize the content in the data dashboard is very important to guarantee comprehension. The best way to do that is by structuring the content from left to right. The most important data points should be placed on the top left corner of the dashboard.

This will allow users to receive the essential details first so they can remember them easily. Having the most important data in the right place; will help users to remember the key data even if they get distracted or skip something.

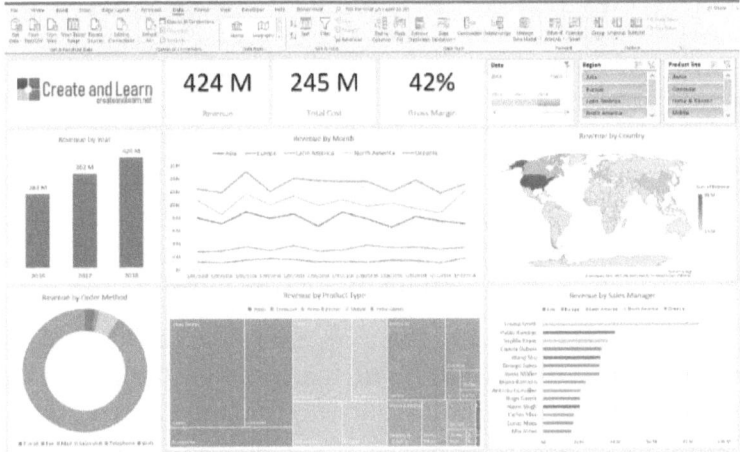

4. The Design Should Be Simple

When it comes to creating an effective data dashboard, the old adage has never been more adequate: "less is more". You want the users of the data dashboard to be free of distractions. If something causes constant distractions, the data will be overlooked and it will defeat the purpose of the data dashboard.

For this reason, you want your data dashboard to have few colors, and fonts so the information is consistent and easier to retain, use few images, use sizing to express which data points are the most important, and use a light theme. The simpler, the better. You want the data dashboard to be all about the data and about the effective communication of metrics. This should be the goal of your design.

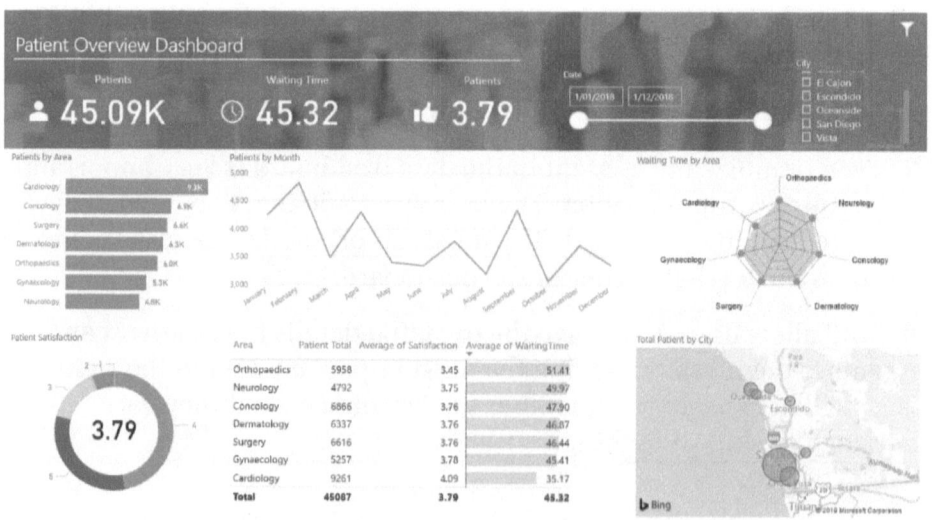

5. Stay Organized

One of the biggest mistakes people make when creating a data dashboard is having the information all over the place. You want your information to be as organized as possible, which is why the best thing you can do is create groups focused on data or specific information.

It's important to group the information in an organized way. This will provide a clear overview of the data and it will make it easy to take in. Plus, it will help you access the right information very easily. Grouping the information will allow users to read the information with ease, digest it a lot better and understand it effortlessly.

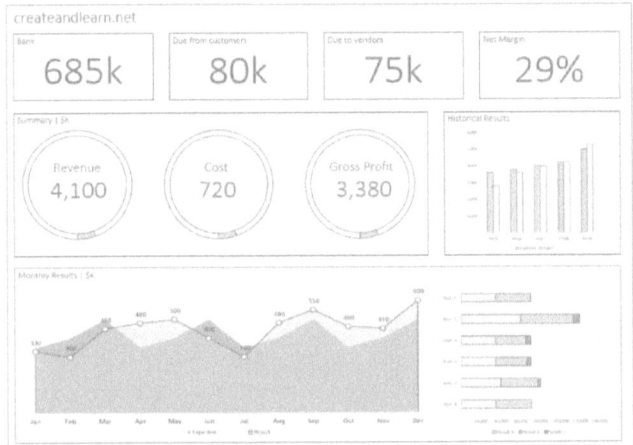

6. Communicate Cause and Effect With Text Blocks

As you can imagine, your business data is all related and it's constantly changing. One thing can affect various data points across your dashboards, so you need a way to understand how data points relate to one another. One of the best ways to do this is to use text blocks to communicate the cause and effect phenomenon between data points.

Text blocks within the data will help you not only understand cause and effect, but it will also allow you to identify different sections and provide a better understanding as to the correlation of the data. Doing this will enable users to understand what the data is communicating.

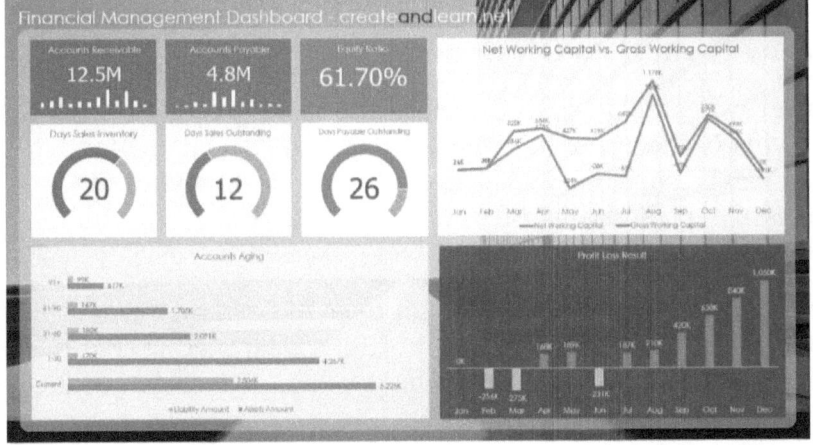

7. Use Widgets and Data Names

Widgets are one of the best tools you can use on your data dashboard. They all come with a default name, which can be either the name of the service that provides the widget or a data set name. However, this can be an issue for many users because they won't understand what's being reported.

To improve that, all you need to do is set up consistent names that easy to understand so users can know what exactly is being reported. This will also make it easy for users to find whatever data points they need. What's important here is that you're consistent with data names; otherwise, they will lead to confusion.

8. Set the Right Time Frames

Data can lie, and it depends on whether you have the wrong time frames. When you're preparing different data points for presentation, each piece of data needs to be set to the same time frame. Otherwise, the data will be corrupted, and it will create confusion.

In some cases, having different time frames is necessary. When that happens, it's vital that the different time frames are outlined and you explain why they're different. If this is not done, you risk having the data be misinterpreted because the people looking at it don't know the time frames are different.

If you want to keep your data honest, make sure the time frames are right and if they need to be different, make sure you inform the users of the data dashboard by making it clear in writing.

9. Keep Away From Data Overload

Data is ever-growing and it's become more and more accessible every day. We're living in the age of information and there's no denying that. As a result, it can be super easy to be overwhelmed by analytics. It's easy to drown in data, and this is true for everyone who works with data.

Remember that a data dashboard is meant to be focused on the data you actually need to analyze so that it can paint a clear picture. For this reason, you should avoid vanity metrics or any kind of data that will distract your data dashboard users. As mentioned above, less is more, and that continues to be true.

Your data dashboard should only report on the data points that are 100% necessary. You need to make sure of this by avoiding data overload. Stick to what's essential for the user of the data dashboard and scale back when you need to, so they only have access to the data that's relevant.

10. Consider the Way the Data Dashboard Will Be Shared

When you're creating a data dashboard to share, you want to take into account how you will be sharing it. Why? Because the way you share your data dashboard can change the structure of it, thus affecting the information in it.

If the data dashboard is presented in person, some text blocks can be left out so you can explain the data yourself. However, that's not always the case. It's more common for data dashboards to be sent to someone else who will view the data on their own. The last thing you want is for the data points to be misinterpreted, so make sure they receive the data dashboard in good condition.

Data Dashboard Design Tips Everyone Should Know

A considerable part of what makes a data dashboard efficient comes down to design. There are many ways to go about it, but here are some essential data dashboard design tips everyone should know about!

1. Stick to What's Essential

When you're creating a data dashboard, it's very tempting to add as many visuals as possible. Images and graphics are definitely a trap. To avoid falling into it, remember that simplicity is key. You don't want to distract or overwhelm the users of the data dashboard. On the contrary, you want users to obtain the right data so you need to stick to what's essential for them and make that the focus of the dashboard without distracting from it.

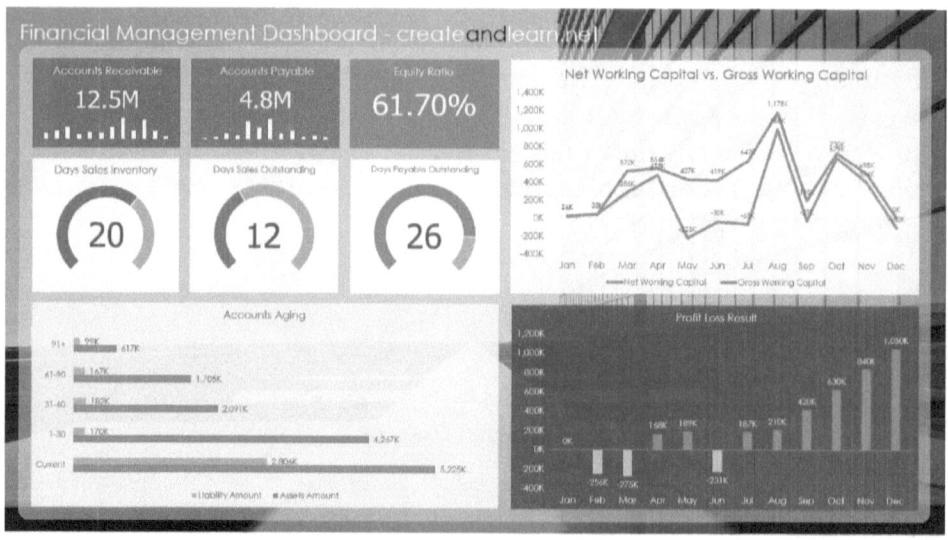

2. Use a Grid Format

Of course, visuals such as charts and images are very important on a data dashboard. The best way to place them is by using a grid layout. This kind of layout will contribute to the reading flow of the data dashboard and it will allow users to guide themselves in a logical way to take in what they need from the dashboard.

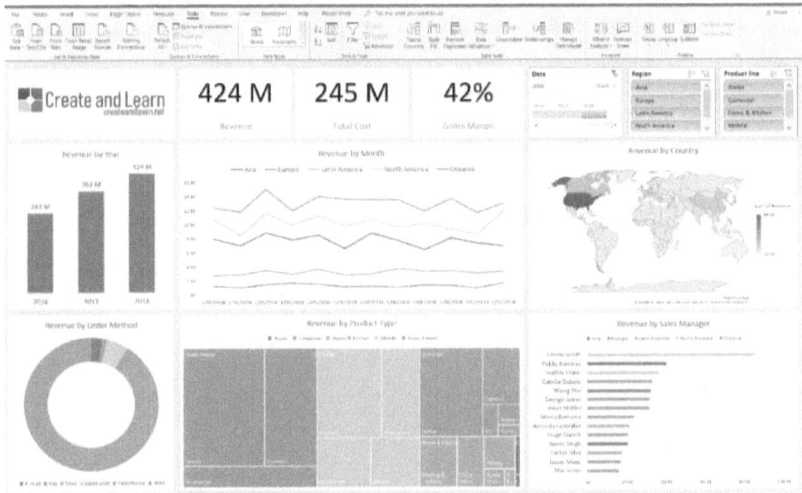

3. Choose the Right Fonts

Typography is a very important element in data dashboard design. It's tempting to use different fonts and sizes. However, you want to use font to create a simple hierarchy. It's recommended you stick to a single font, but if you decide to use more than one, make sure you don't overdo it.

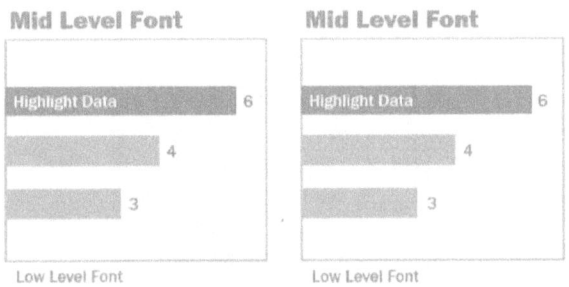

4. Do not Use Too Much Color

Using too many different colors on your data dashboard won't add to the value of it. In fact, it will reduce it. Using many colors in a single space creates distraction and it can be very confusing. You want to work with color palettes that are pleasant. But above all, don't use too many colors.

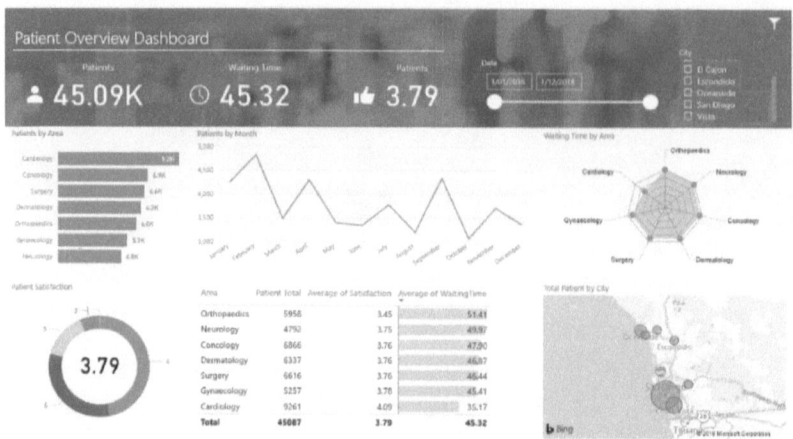

5. Big Numbers

Data dashboards are all about showing users the most important information in a way that's easy to take in. This is why you want to avoid big numbers. Instead of showing $57,213,324.01, go with $57.2M. It's short, to the point, and it provides the necessary information.

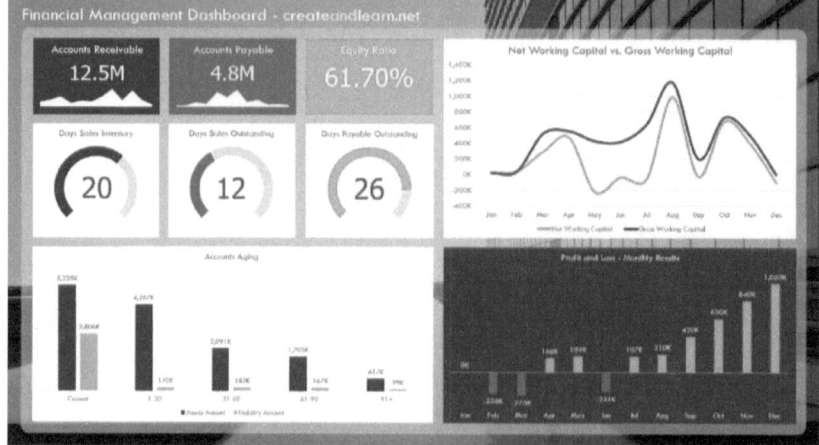

6. Use the Right Charts

There are many different kinds of charts available and they each serve a different purpose. When you're creating your data dashboard, you want to make sure you use the right charts for the right purposes. This way, you'll make sure visualization is as effective as can be.

For example, line charts are great for displaying change patterns across a continuum. They're clear, compact and precise. What's more, they are easy to analyze at a glance, which is beneficial for many data points.

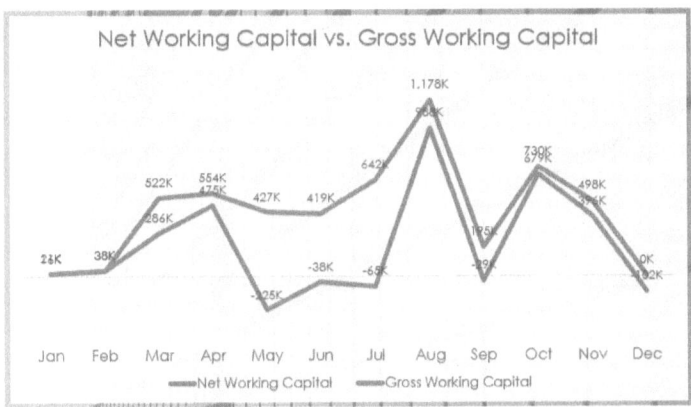

Bar charts are great for when users want to compare items in a category easily and quickly. This type of chart is also clear, compact and precise, which makes it very easy to understand.

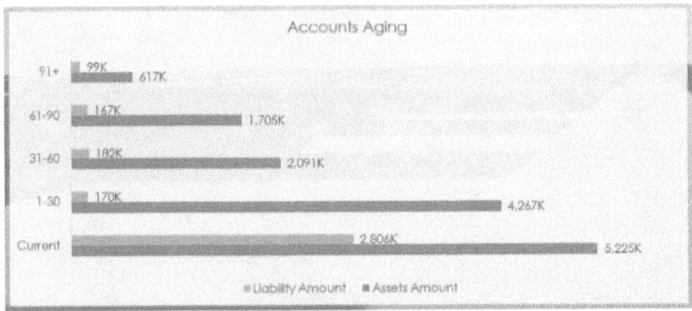

Although Pie charts and Doughnut charts have been criticized by some people that argue it is difficult to compare different sections, they are largely used in the mass media and business world. They can be handy and tell a good story if you take care to include data labels and not to use more than five sections and

17

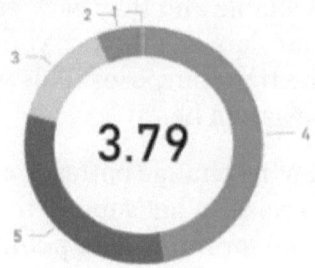

Patient Satisfaction

3.79

These are only a few of the most popular charts, there are many more. What you need to keep in mind for data dashboards that focus on charts and visualization is that the chart type you use will depend on what you want to communicate.

4. The Financial Management Dashboard

The people who work in finance need to deal with large amounts do data. Keeping track of all information, KPIs (key performance indicators) and data that department is responsible, can be overwhelming, and a great tool to help with this task is a Dashboard by showing all the critical information in one location.

In the chapters below, you will follow all the steps to create a Financial Management Dashboard, using Microsoft Excel and the fundamentals of Dashboard Designing.

5. Getting the Data File

1- Visit the address https://www.createandlearn.net/easy1

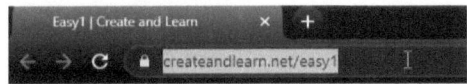

2- Download the file **1 – Financial Dashboard – Data.xlsx** . This file contains the data and image that you will use to create the Dashboard.

3- When you open the file click **Enable Editing** if Excel asks.

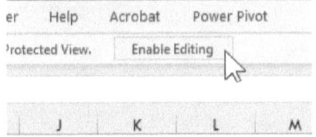

6.Preparing the Dashboard

1- If you want to save this file in a diffent folder, go to **File** tab and click on **Save As**. Choose a folder and save the file.

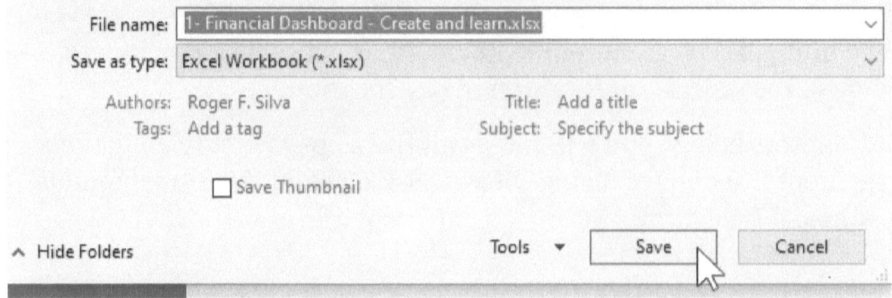

2- Go to the sheet **Image**.

3- Click on the image to select it. Then, go to **Home** tab and click on **Copy**.

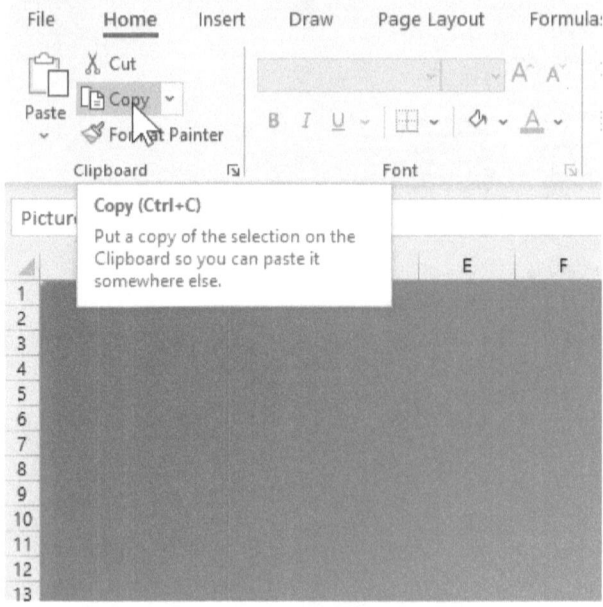

4- Go to **Dashboard** sheet

5- Click on cell A1, go to **Home** tab and select **Paste**.

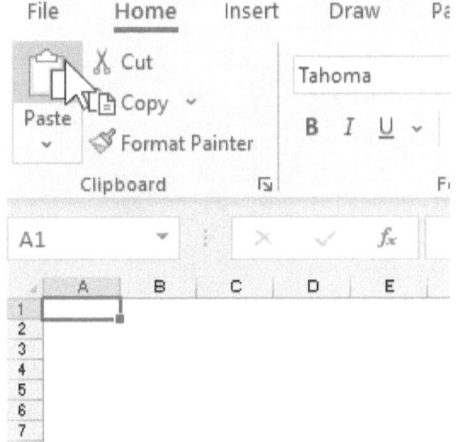

6- Thag and drop the background picture to be similar to the image below.

7- Excel offers themes that allow you to change the look and feeling of your workbook. Go to **Page Layout** tab, click on **Themes** and select the **Circuit** theme.

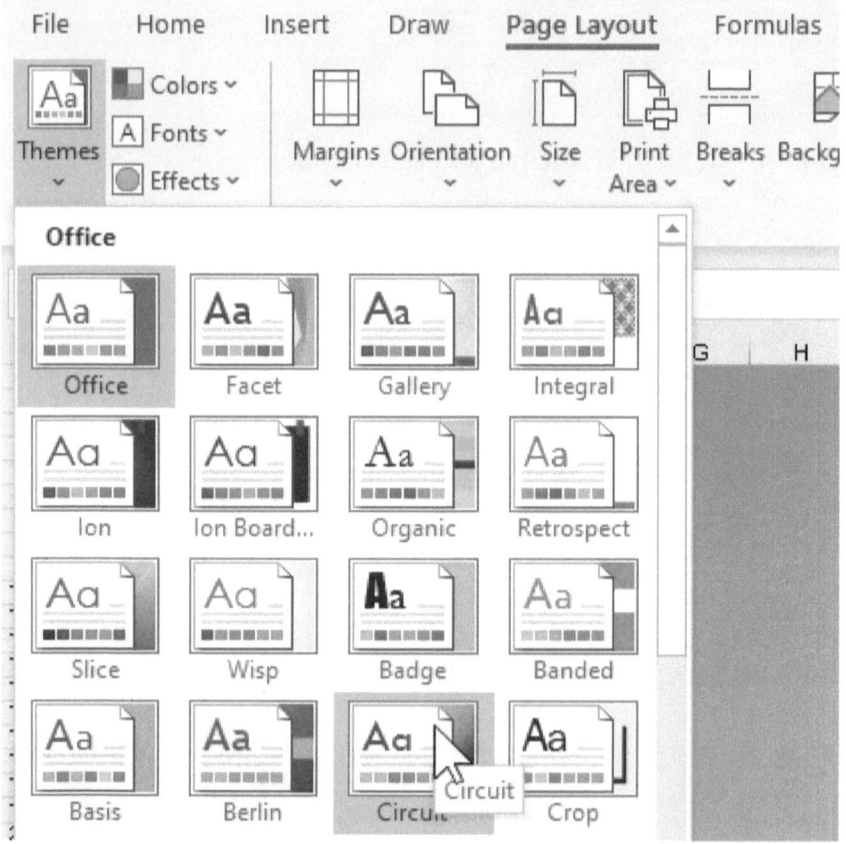

Learn more about Excel Themes and how to customize them in this article: https://www.createandlearn.net/post/excel-appearance

8- Go to **Insert** tab, click on **Shapes**, and select **Rectangle: Rounded Corners**.

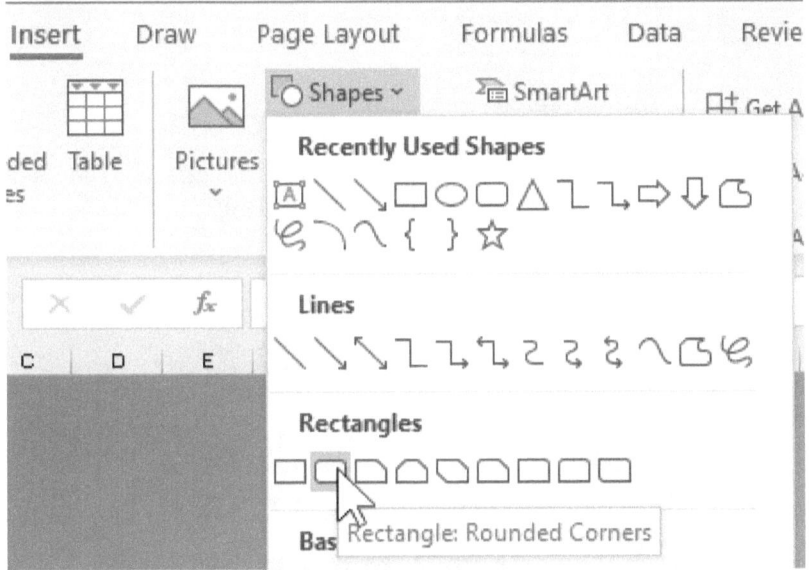

9- Click and drag to draw the rectangle like the image below.

10- Click and drag the yellow handle at the top to reduce the curvature.

11- With the rectangle selected, go to **Shape Format** and change the **Shape Fill** color to **Dark Blue, Text 2, Lighter 80%**.

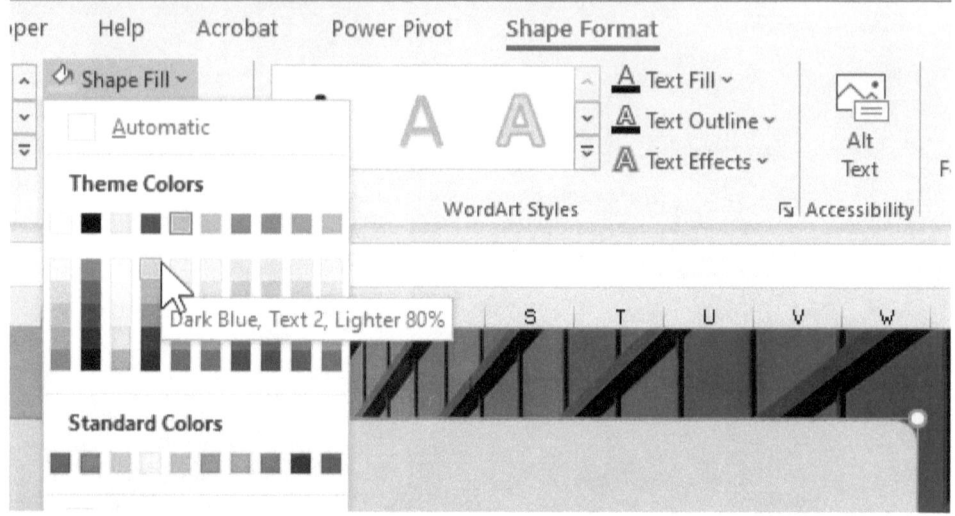

12- Go back to the **Shape Fill** and click on **More Fill Colors**.

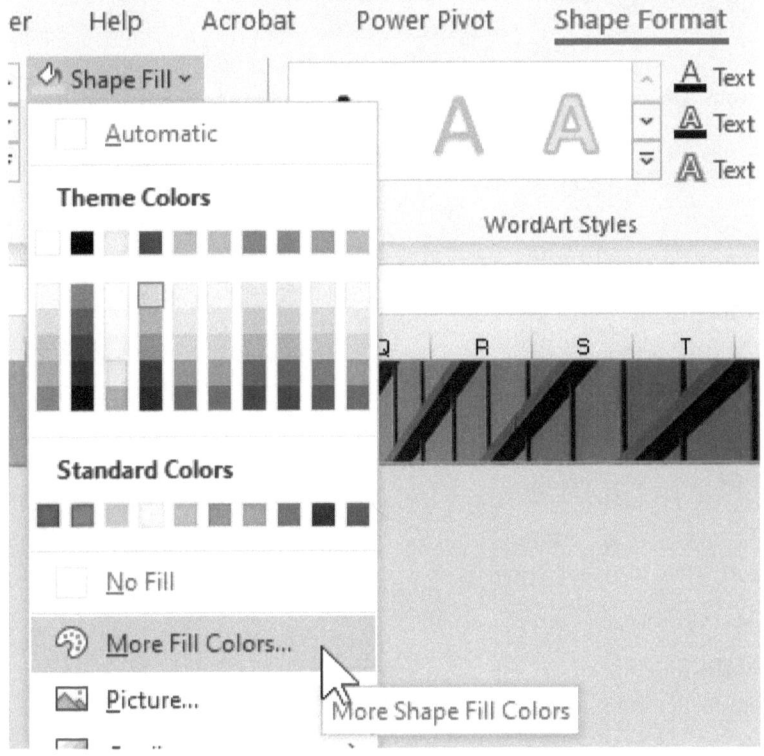

13- Change the **Transparency** to 50% and click **OK.**

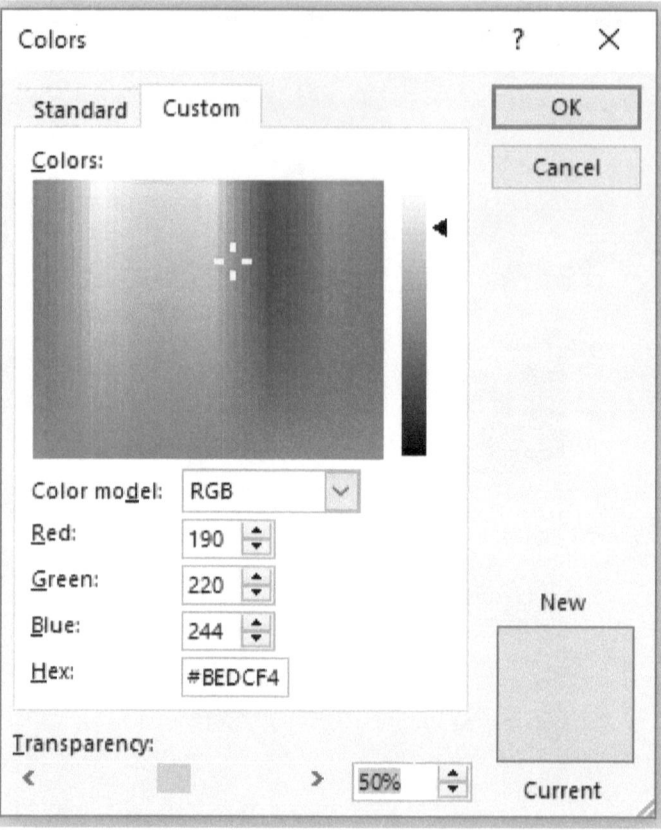

14- With the rectangle selected, go to **Shape Format** tab, **Shape Outline**, and click on **No Outline**.

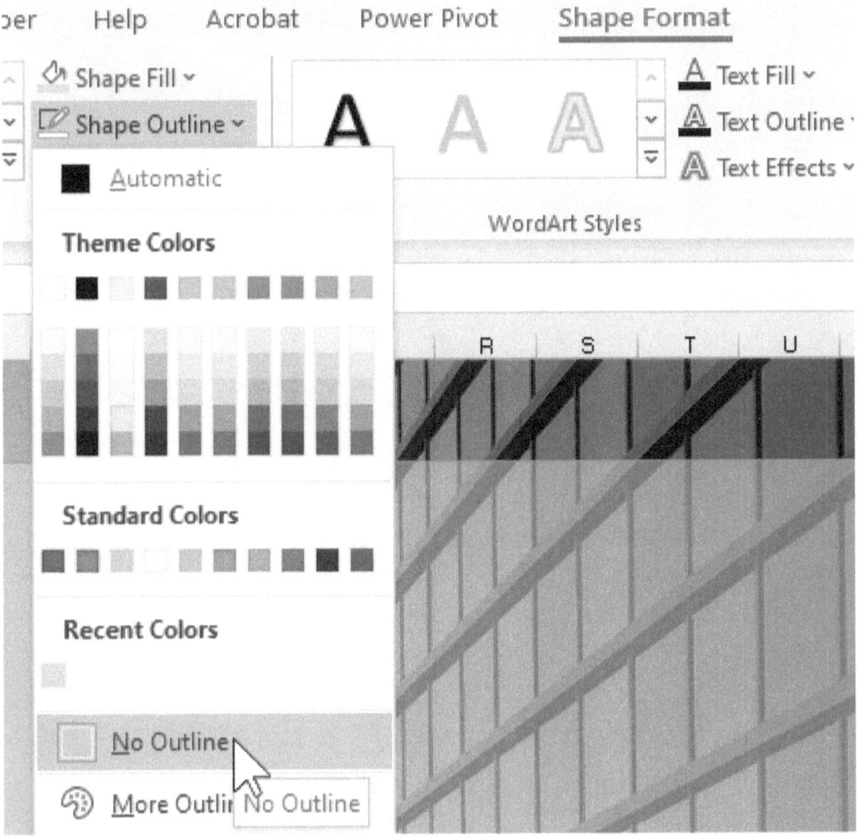

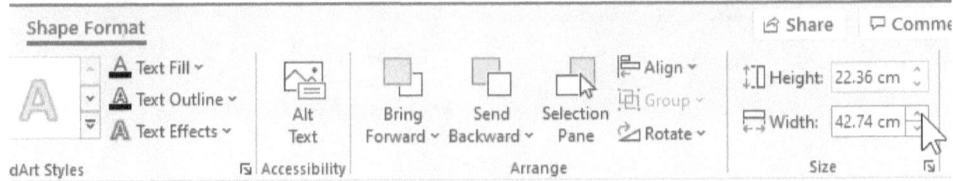

15- Go to **Shape Format** tab and change the **Height** to 22.36 cm, and the **Width** to 42.74 cm.

16- Go to **Insert** and click on **Text Box**.

17- Click on the top of the dashboard to activate the text box and type the dashboard title: **Financial Management Dashboard - createandlearn.net**

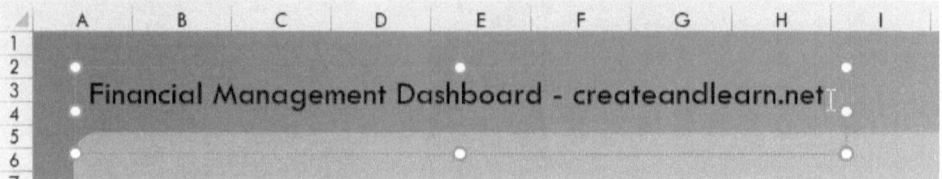

18- Select the text box. Then, Go to **Home** tab, and change the **Font** color to **White, Background 1**.

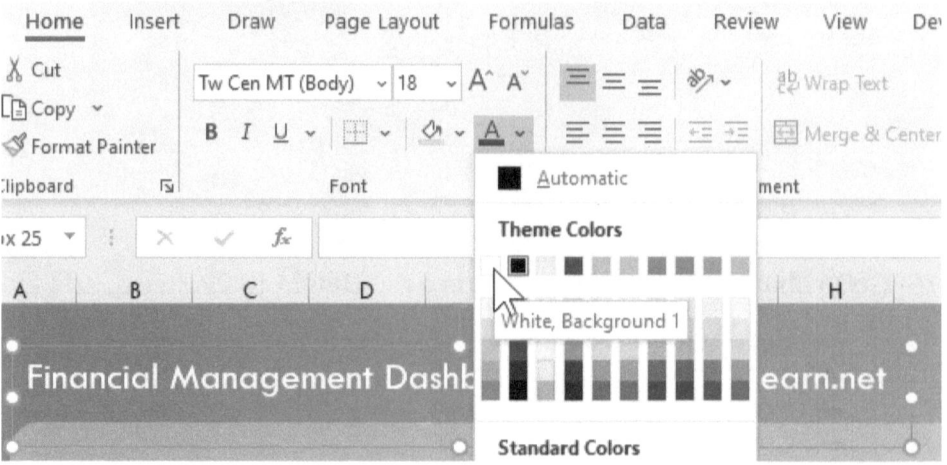

19- Highlight the word **"and"**. Then, change the font color to **Sky Blue, Background 2**.

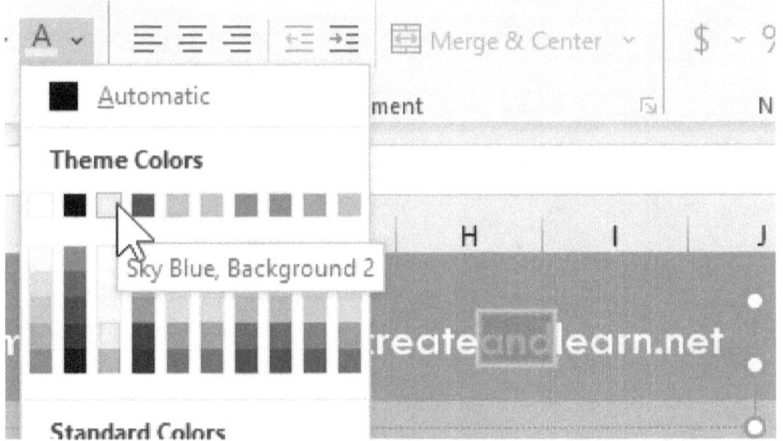

20- Change the **Font Size** to 28.

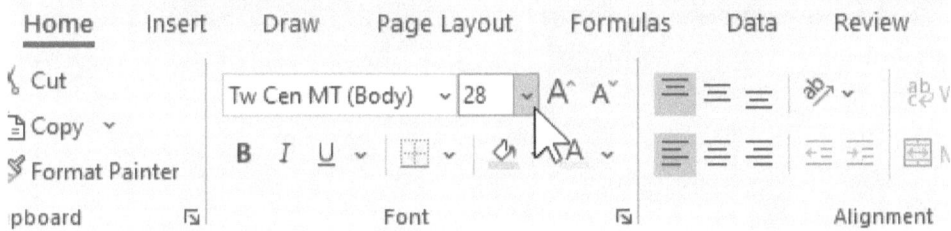

21- Drag and drop the objects to have a Dashboard like the image below.

7.Showing the Big Numbers

1- Go to the **Accounts Receivable** sheet.

2- Select the cells range **A1:B13**.

A1		× ✓ fx	Date

◢	A	B	C
1	Date	Accounts Receivable	
2	Jan	651K	
3	Feb	874K	
4	Mar	1,300K	
5	Apr	500K	
6	May	791K	
7	Jun	686K	
8	Jul	1,295K	
9	Aug	2,249K	
10	Sep	868K	
11	Oct	2,100K	
12	Nov	866K	
13	Dec	335	
14	Total	12,514K	
15			

3- Go to **Insert** tab, **Charts** and select the **Area** chart.

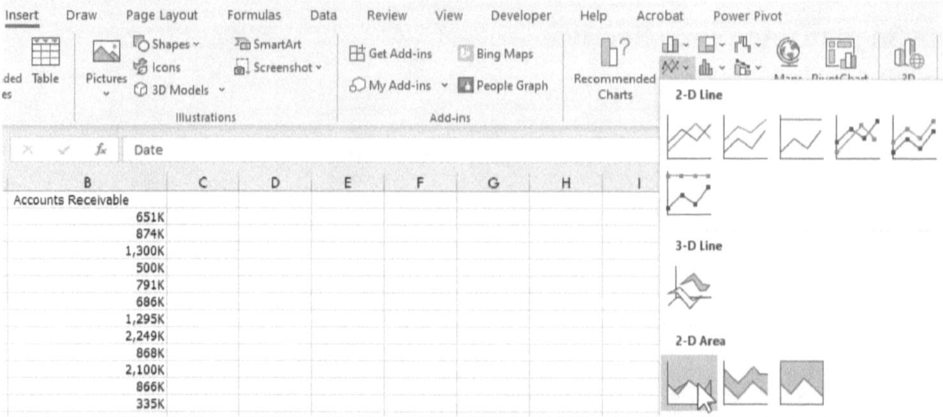

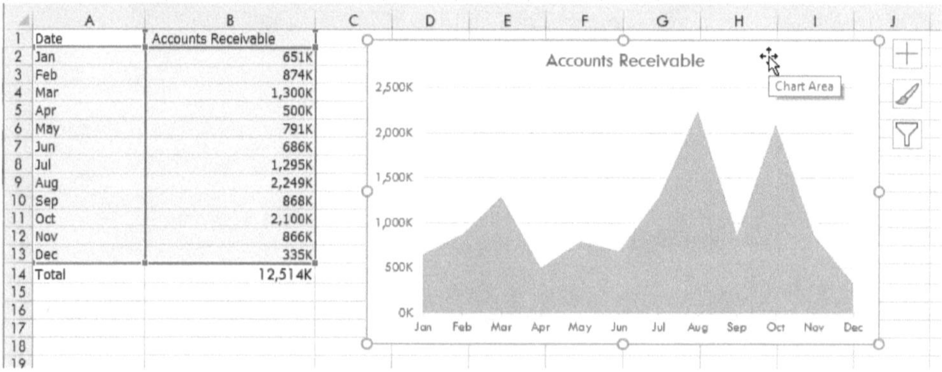

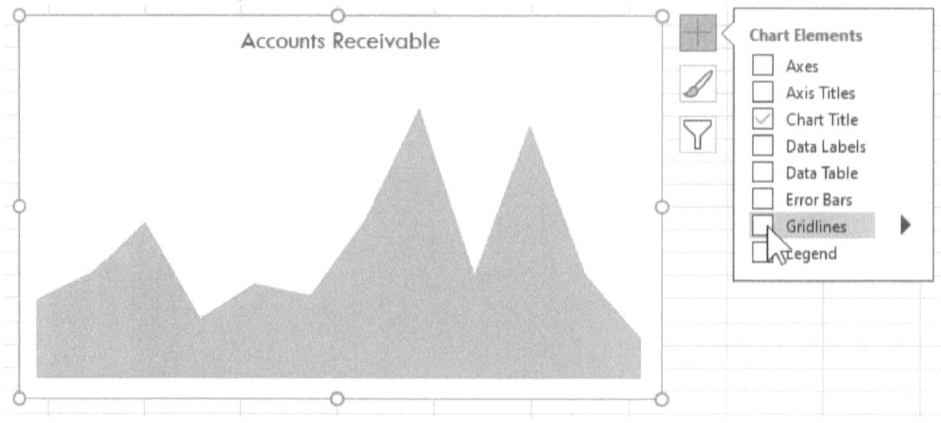

4- With the chart selected click on **Chart Elements** ("+" icon). Then, uncheck **Gridlines**, and **Axes**.

5- Go to **Format** tab, **Shape Outline**, and click on **No Outline**.

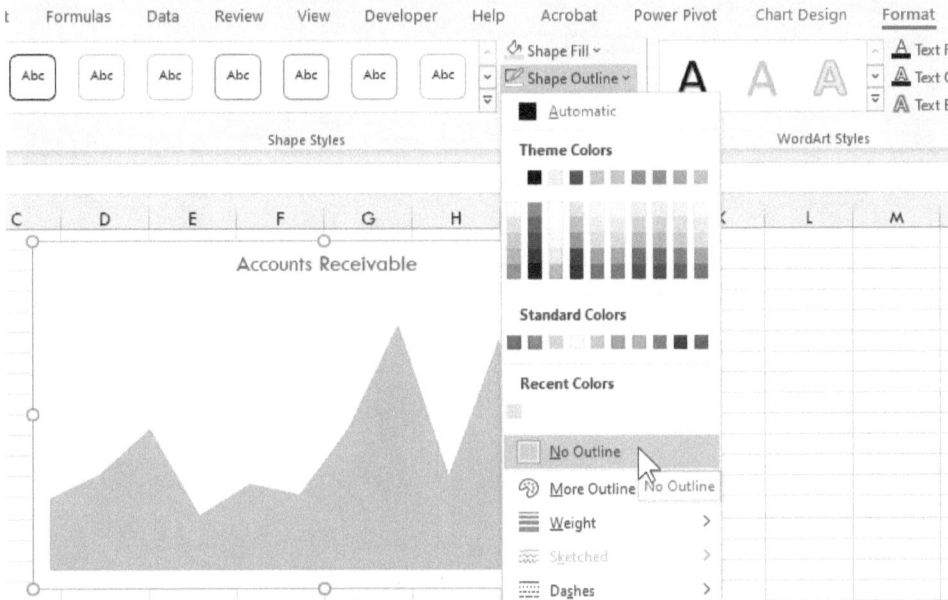

6- Right-click the **Chart Area** and click on **Move Chart**.

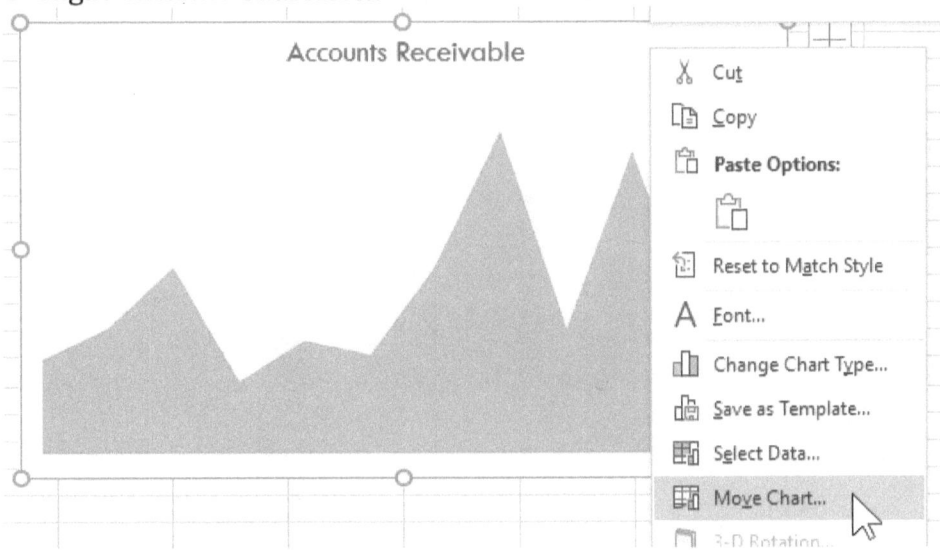

7- Check the option **Object in**, select **Dashboard**, and click OK.

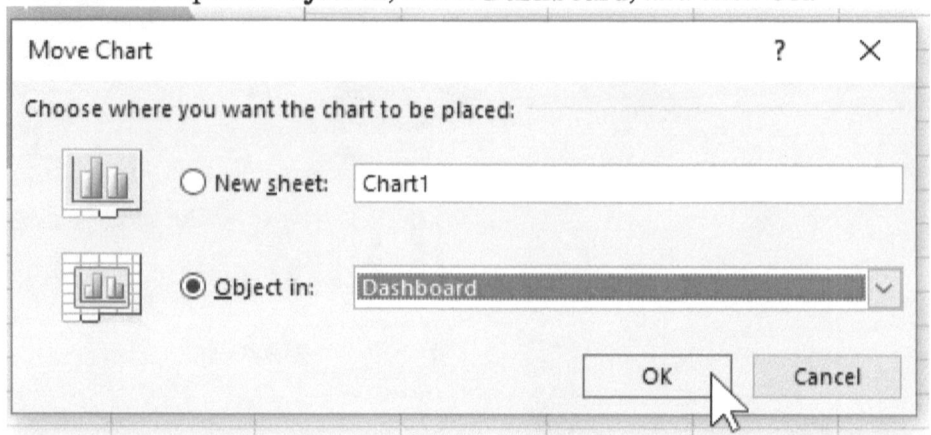

8- Select the chart. go to **Format** tab and change the **Height** to 4.17 cm, and the **Width** to 6.95 cm.

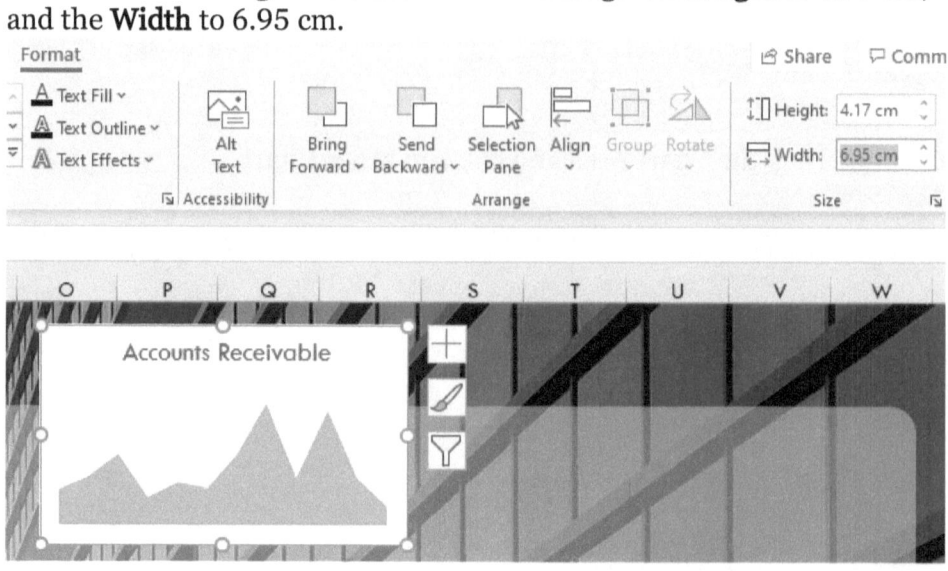

9- With the **chart** selected, go to **Format** tab, and change the **Shape Fill** color to **Dark Blue, Text 2, Darker 25%**.

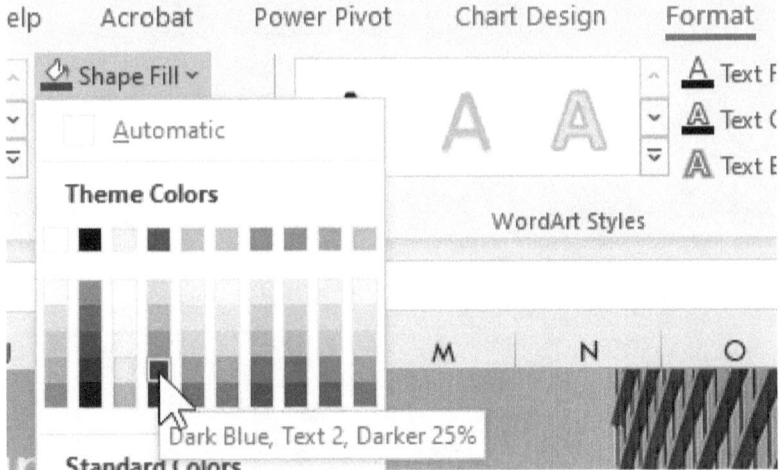

10- Change the **Text Fill** color to **White, Background 1**.

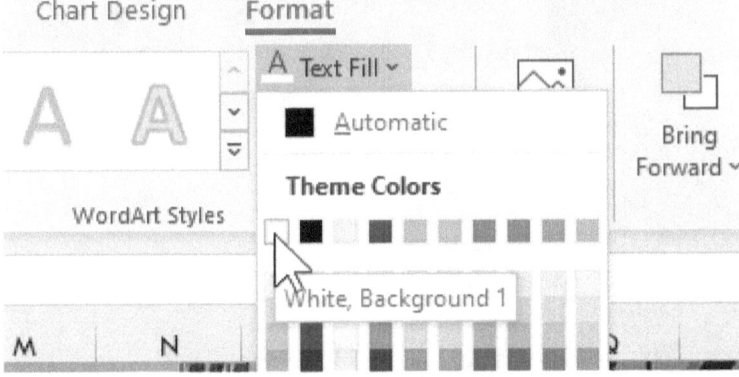

11- With the **series** selected, go to **Format** tab, and change the **Shape Fill** color to **White, Background 1**.

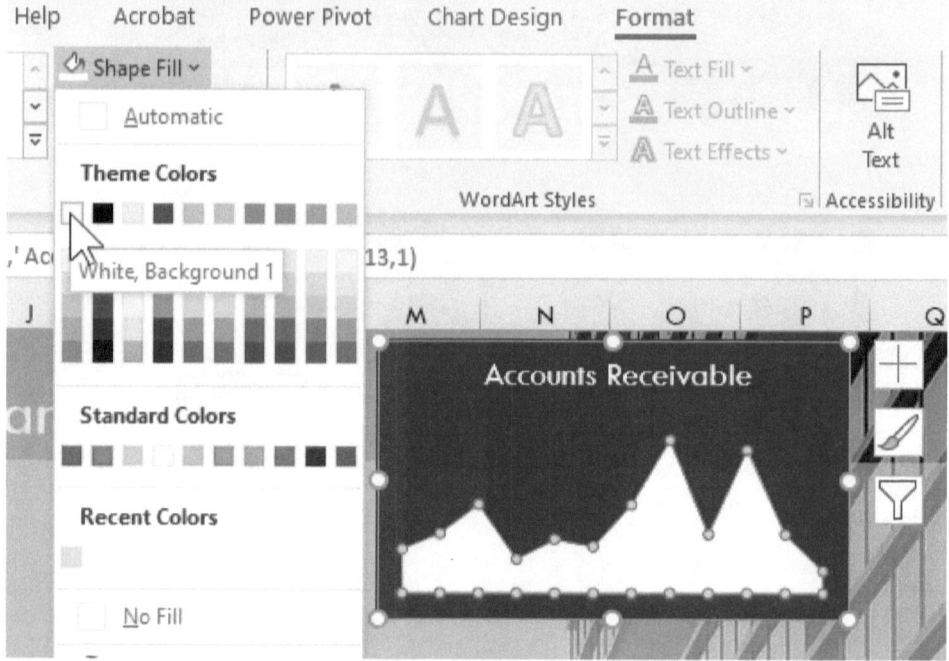

12- Click over the **Plot Area** to activate it.

13- Click and drag to reduce the size of the Plot Area only.

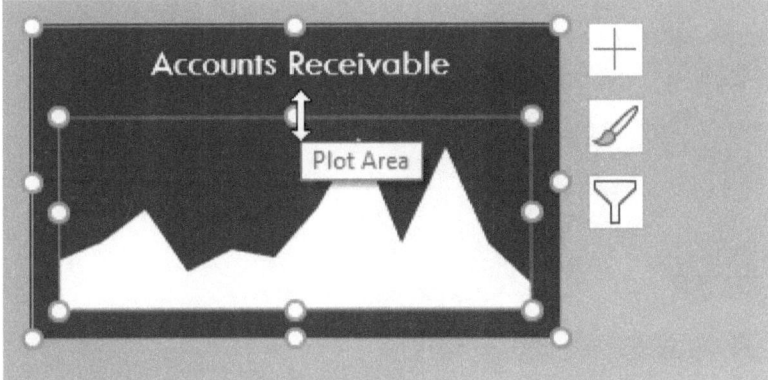

14- Reduce the Plot Area to approximately 50% of the original.

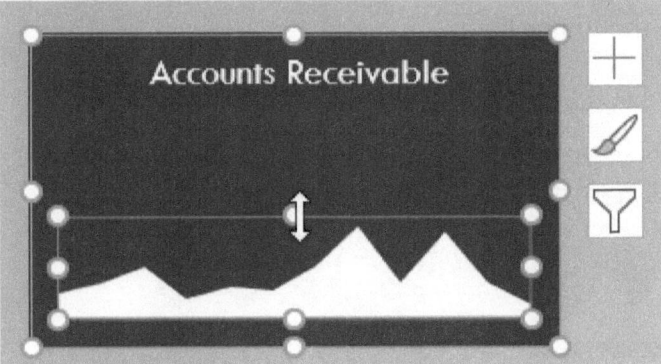

15- With the chart selected go to **Format** tab, **Shape Outline**, and click on **No Outline**. Then, Right-click the **Chart** and click on **Copy**.

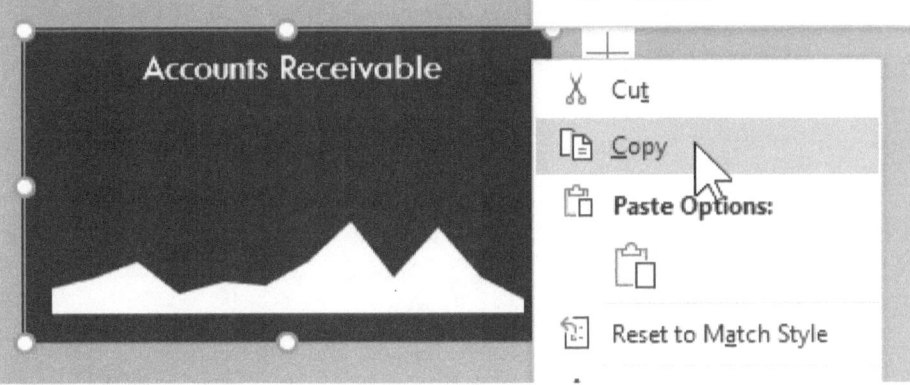

16- Click on the background to deselect the chart, right-click and select **Paste**.

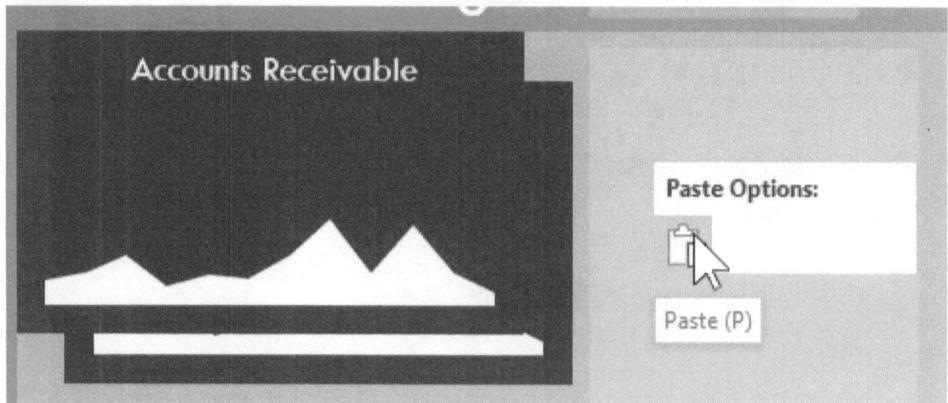

17- Move the chart as the image below.

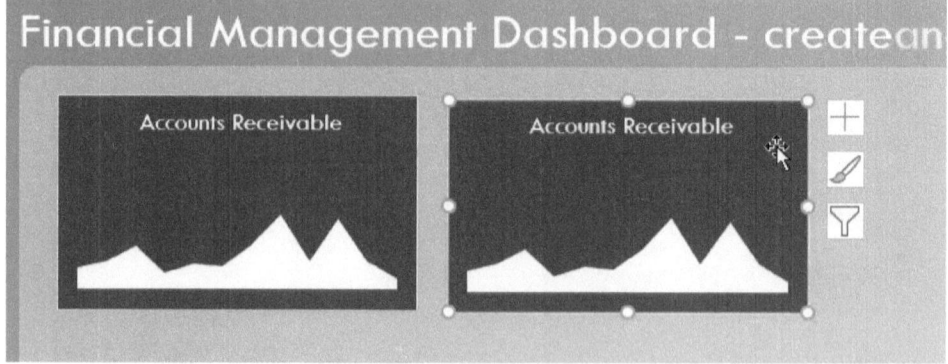

18- With the new chart selected, go to **Home** tab, and change the **Fill** color to **Red, Accent 3, Darker 25%.**

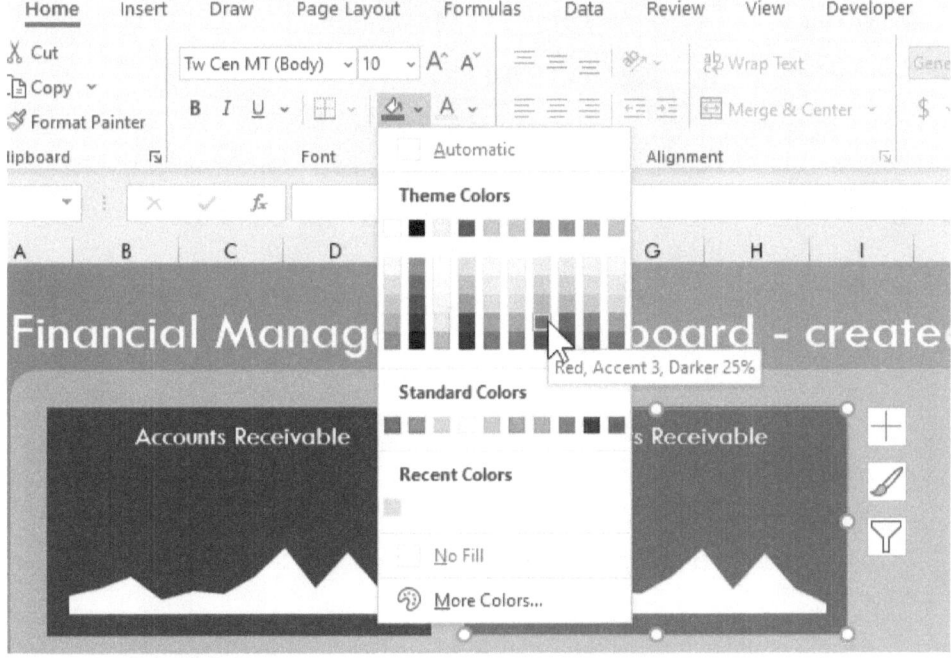

19- Go to **Chart Design** tab and click on **Select Data**.

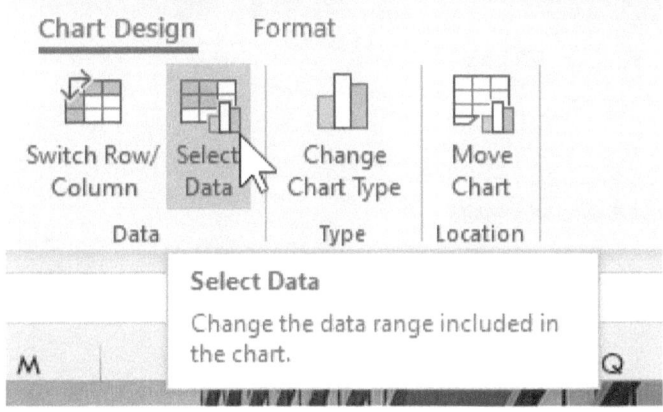

20- Change the **Chart data range** to **=' Accounts Payable'!$A$1:$B$13**. Then, click **OK**.

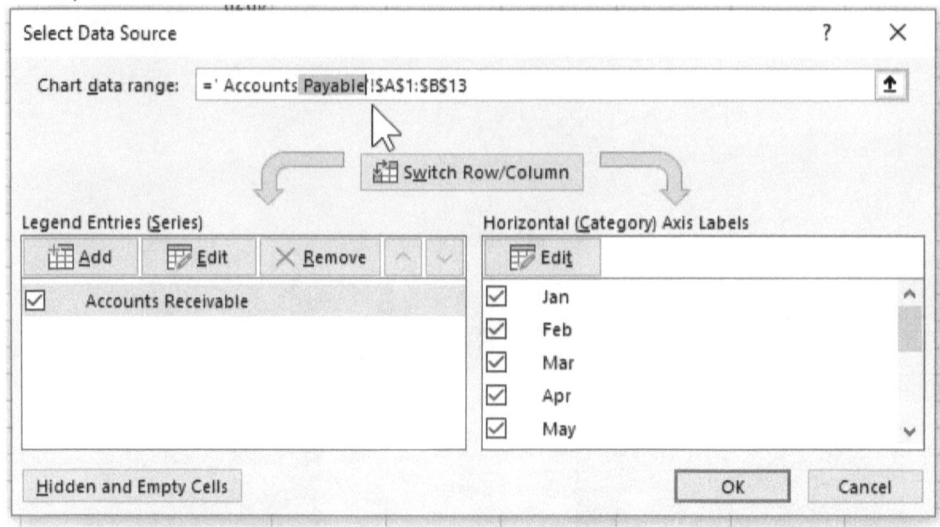

21- Go to **Insert** tab and add a new **Text Box**.

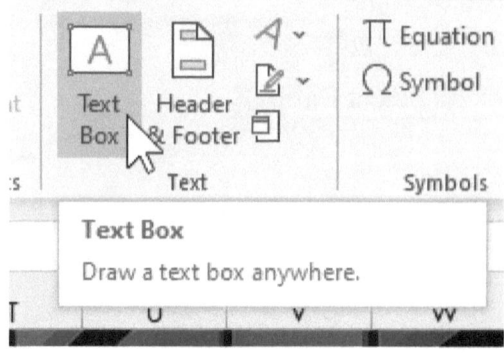

22- With the text box selected, type "=" in the **formula bar**, to start creating a link to a cell.

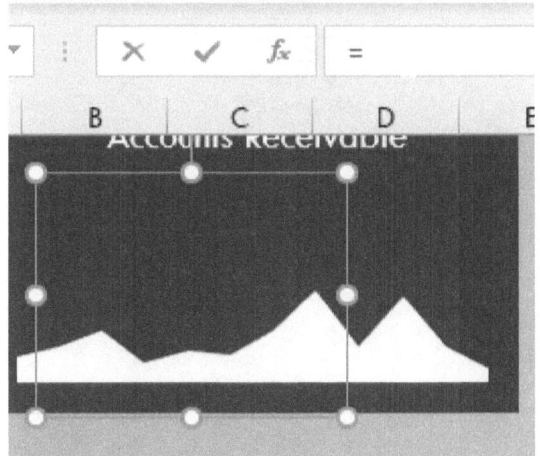

23- Go to **Accounts Receivable** sheet and click on cell **B14**, this will add the cell address to the text box formula. Then, press **Enter**.

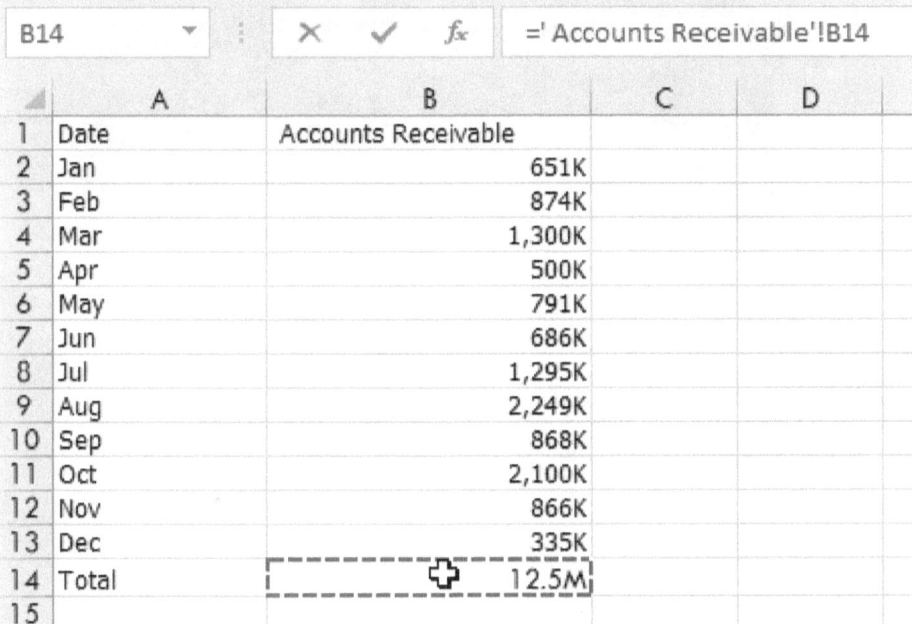

	A	B	C	D
1	Date	Accounts Receivable		
2	Jan	651K		
3	Feb	874K		
4	Mar	1,300K		
5	Apr	500K		
6	May	791K		
7	Jun	686K		
8	Jul	1,295K		
9	Aug	2,249K		
10	Sep	868K		
11	Oct	2,100K		
12	Nov	866K		
13	Dec	335K		
14	Total	12.5M		
15				

B14 formula bar: =' Accounts Receivable'!B14

24- With eh text box selected change the font to **Tahoma**, the size to **32**, the font color to **White** and **Center** alignment.

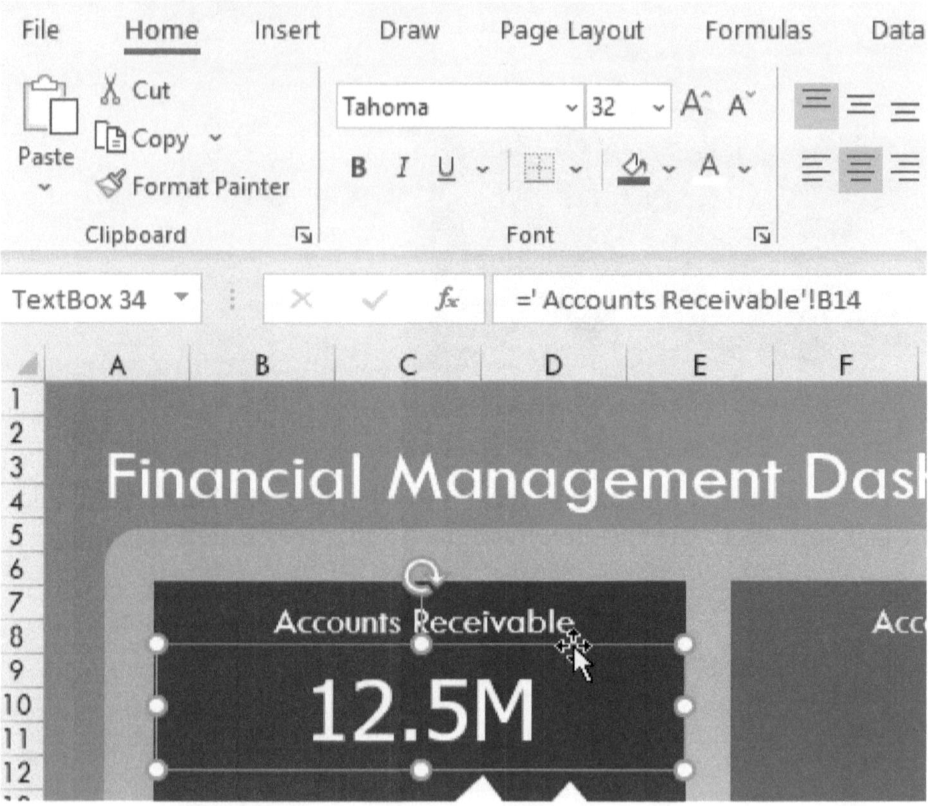

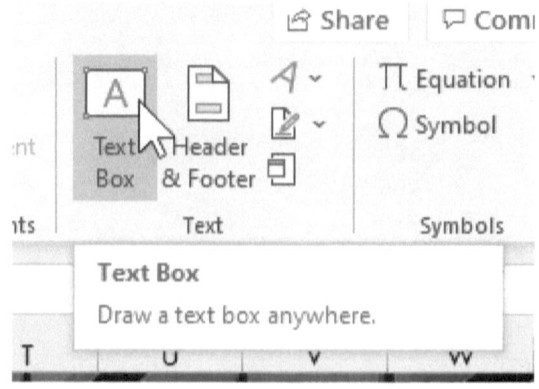

25- Add a new text box.

26- With the text box selected, type "=" in the formula bar, to start creating a link to a cell.

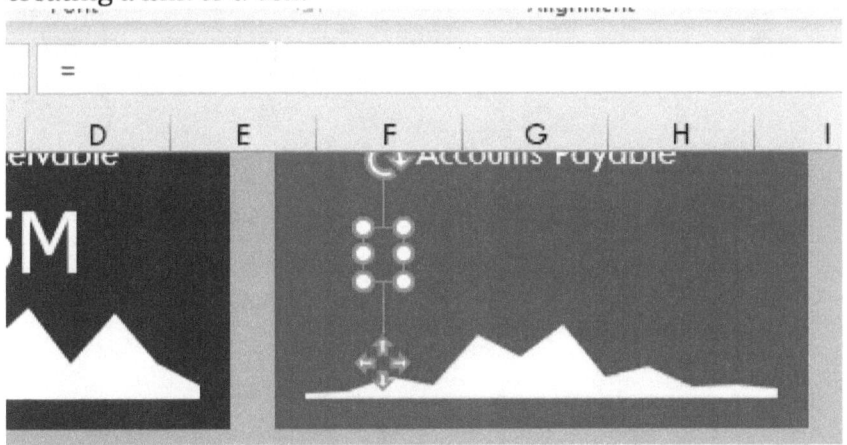

27- Go to **Accounts Payable** sheet and click on cell **B14**, this will add cell address to the text box formula. Then, press **Enter**.

| | B14 | ▼ | ⋮ | ✕ | ✓ | fx | =' Accounts Payable'!B14 |

	A	B	C	D
1	Date	Accounts Payable		
2	Jan	96K		
3	Feb	131K		
4	Mar	331K		
5	Apr	205K		
6	May	952K		
7	Jun	640K		
8	Jul	1,093K		
9	Aug	325K		
10	Sep	483K		
11	Oct	182K		
12	Nov	207K		
13	Dec	147K		
14	Total	4.8M		
15				

28- Select the Accounts Receivable text box. Then click on **Format Painter** to copy the text box style.

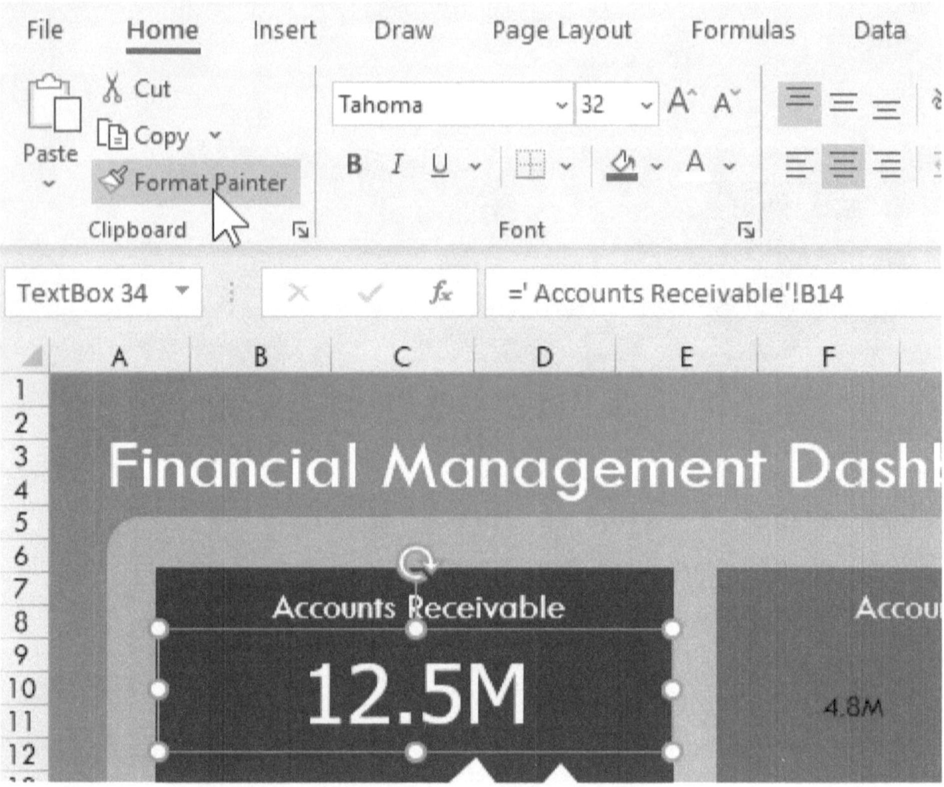

| File | Home | Insert | Draw | Page Layout | Formulas | Data |

Tahoma | 32 | A˄ A˅

Paste — Cut, Copy, Format Painter

Clipboard | Font

TextBox 34 | fx | =' Accounts Receivable'!B14

| | A | B | C | D | E | F |

Financial Management Dashl

Accounts Receivable

12.5M

Accou

4.8M

29- Click on the Accounts Payable text box to paste the style.

30- Move the objects to have them like the image below.

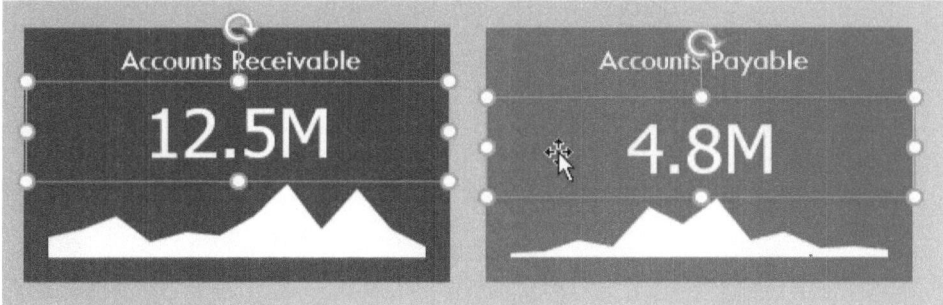

31- To align the text boxes, you can use the align tool. Hold **ctrl** key and click on both text boxes. Release the ctrl key. Then, go to **Shape Format**, click on **Align** and choose the alignment that makes sense to you need, in this example was used **Align Top**.

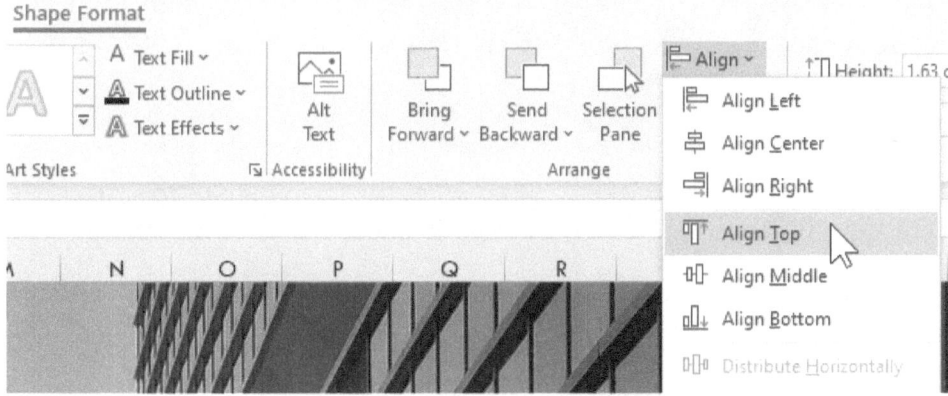

32- The dashboard should look like the image below.

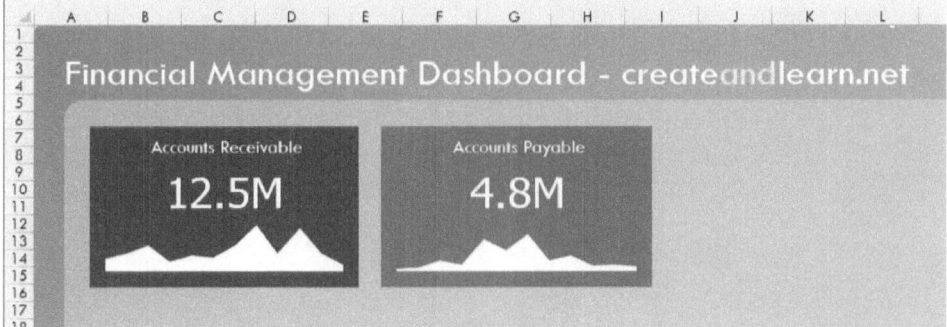

33- Add a new text box at the right of the Accounts Payable card..

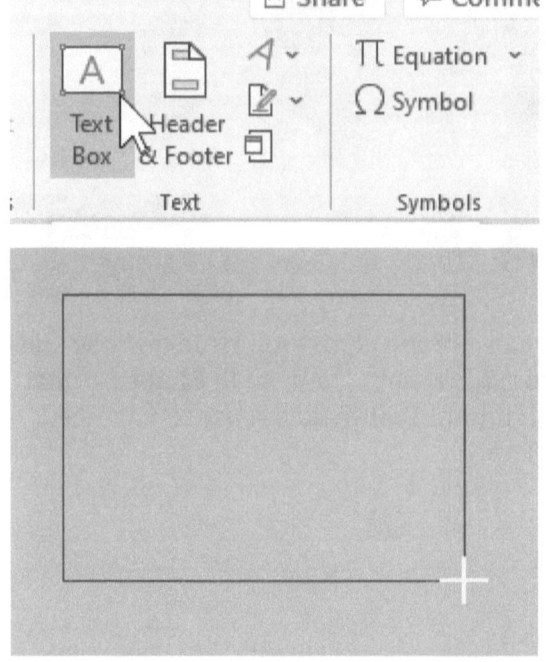

34- With the text box selected, type "=" in the formula bar, to start creating a link to a cell. Then, go to KPIS sheet and click on cell B5. Press Enter.

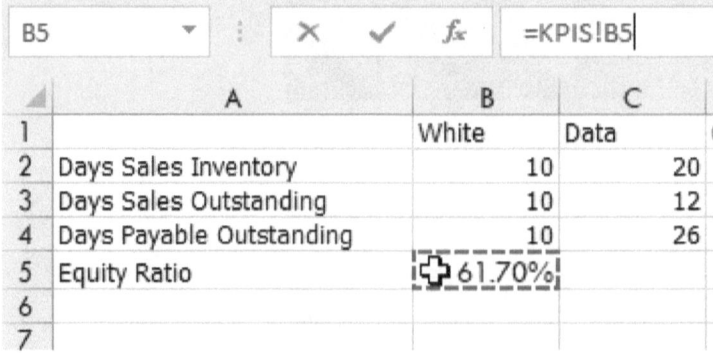

	A	B	C	
1		White	Data	
2	Days Sales Inventory	10	20	
3	Days Sales Outstanding	10	12	
4	Days Payable Outstanding	10	26	
5	Equity Ratio	61.70%		
6				
7				

35- With the text box selected, go to **Shape Format** tab, and change the **Height** to 4.17 cm, and the **Width** to 6.95 cm.

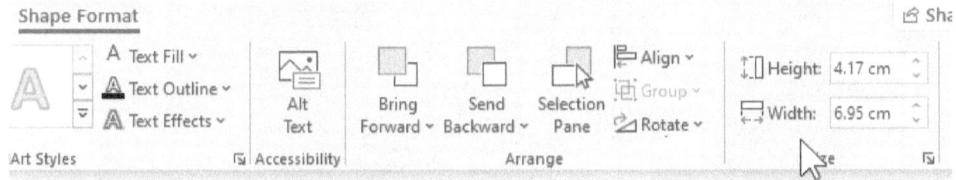

36- Go to **Shape Format** tab, **Shape Outline**, and click on **No Outline**.

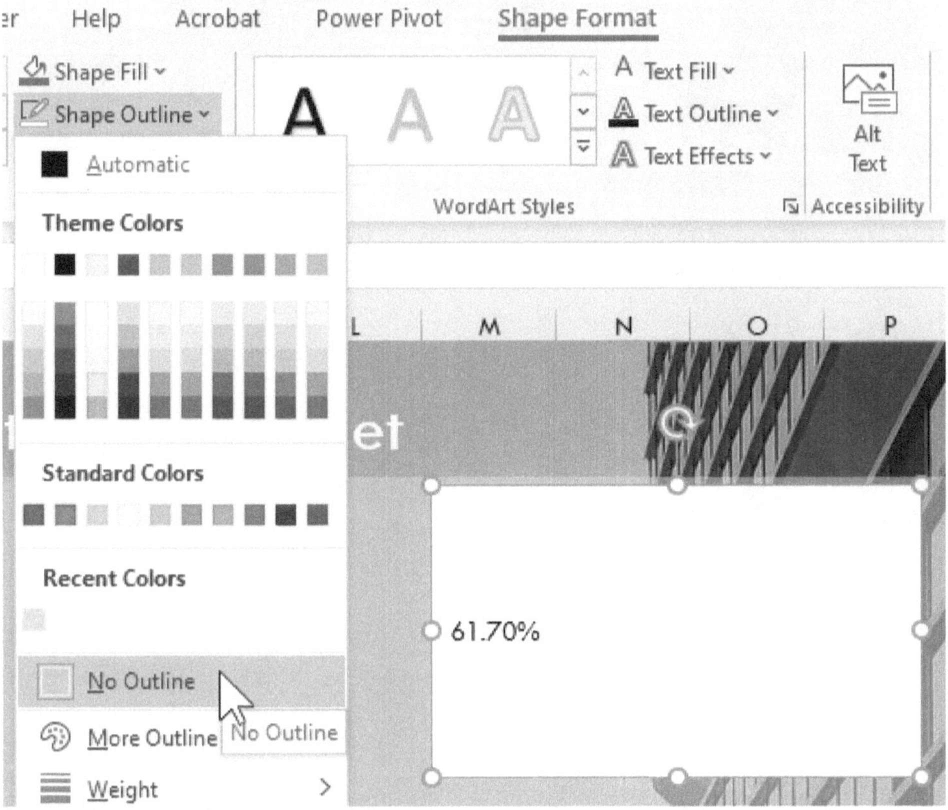

37- With the text box selected, go to **Home** tab, and change the **Fill** color to **Sky Blue, Background 2, Darker 50%**. Change the **Font Size** to 40, the **Font Color** to White, Background 1 and **Alignment** Center, and

Middle.

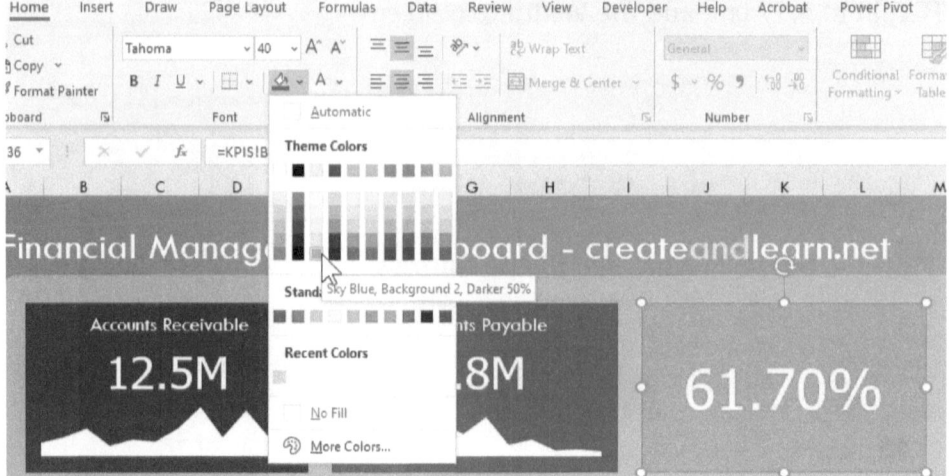

38- To create a title for this new card, go to **Insert** tab add a new text box.

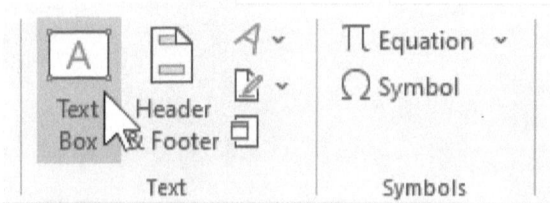

39- Type **Equity Ratio**, and change the font size to **18,** the color to **white,** and **Center** alignment..

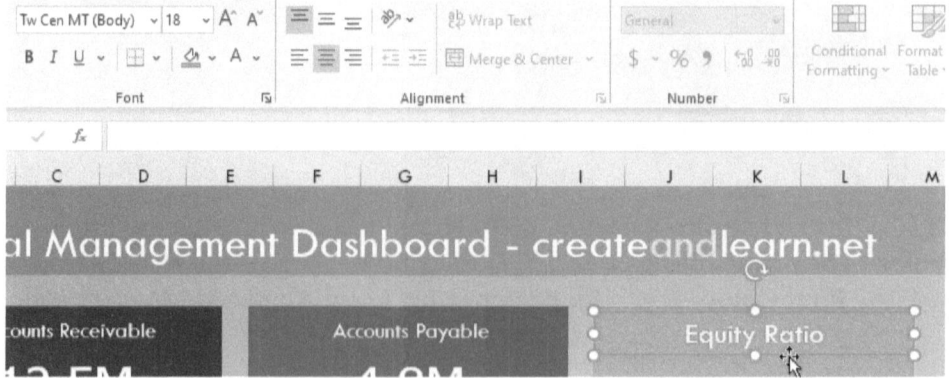

40- Be sure to have the three titles with font size **18**.

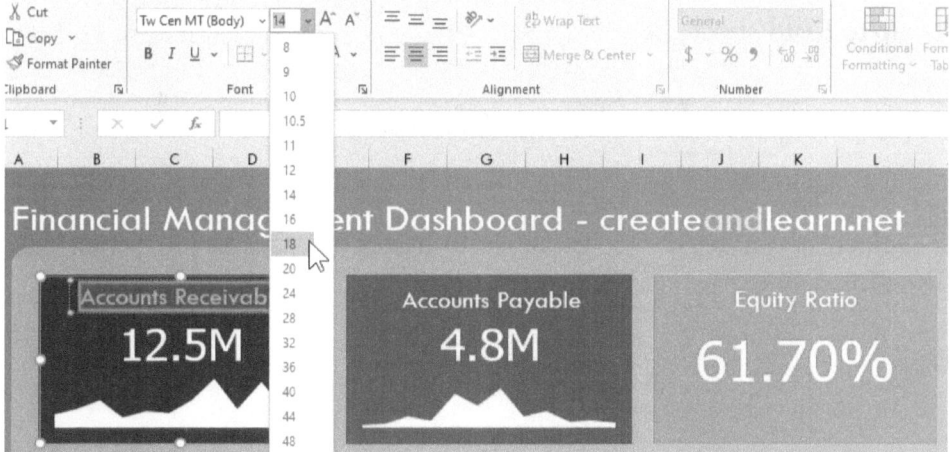

41- Drag and drop the objects to have a Dashboard like the image below.

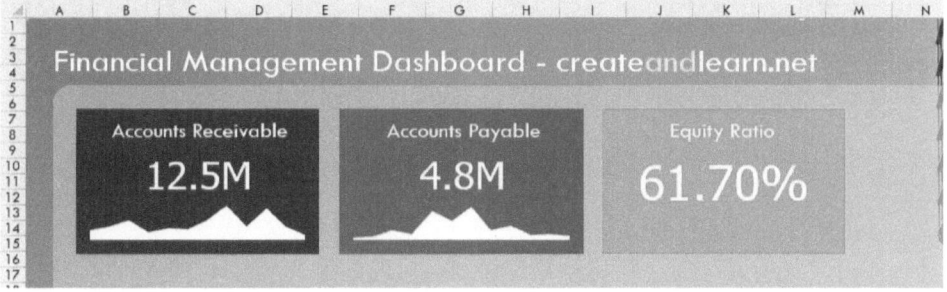

8.Working with Doughnut charts

1- Go to **KPIS** sheet.

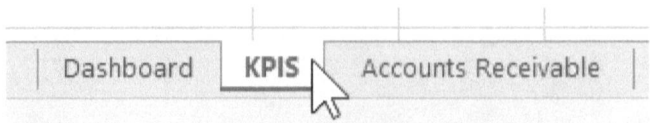

2- Select the range **A2:D2**. Then, Go to **Insert** tab, **Charts** and select the **Doughnut** chart.

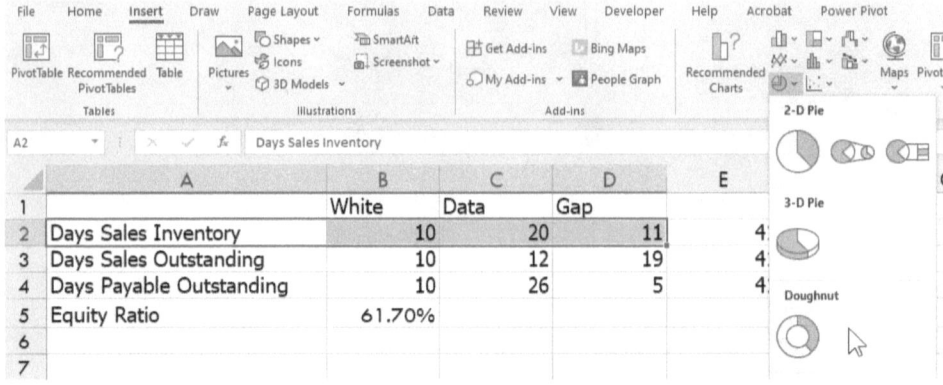

3- Right-click any data series and click on **Format Data Series**.

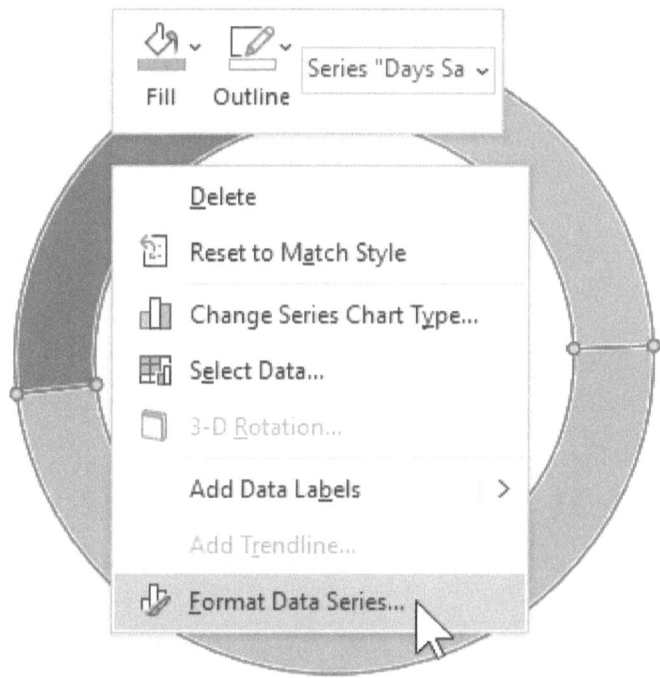

4- Go to **Series Options** and set the **Angle of first slice** to 137.

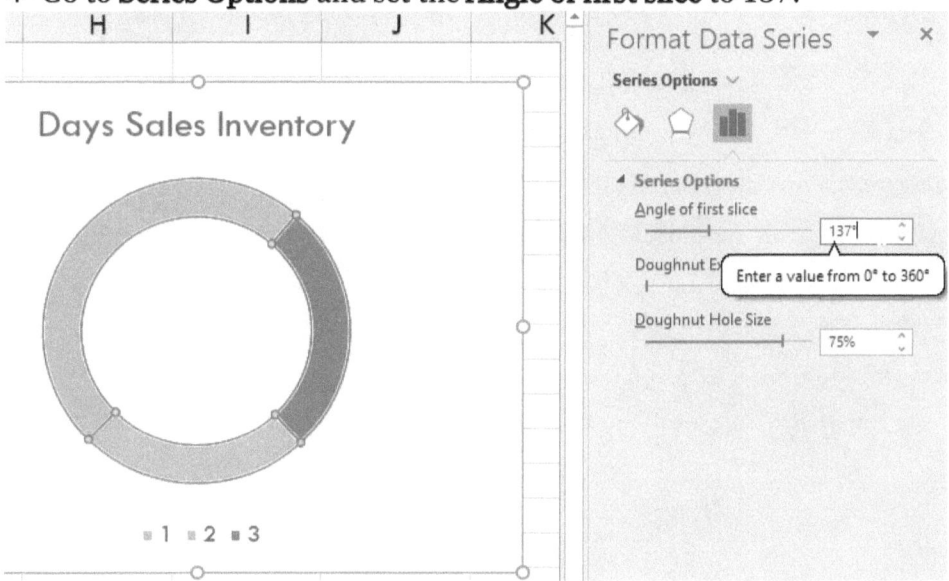

5- Double click the **Point 1** to single select it.

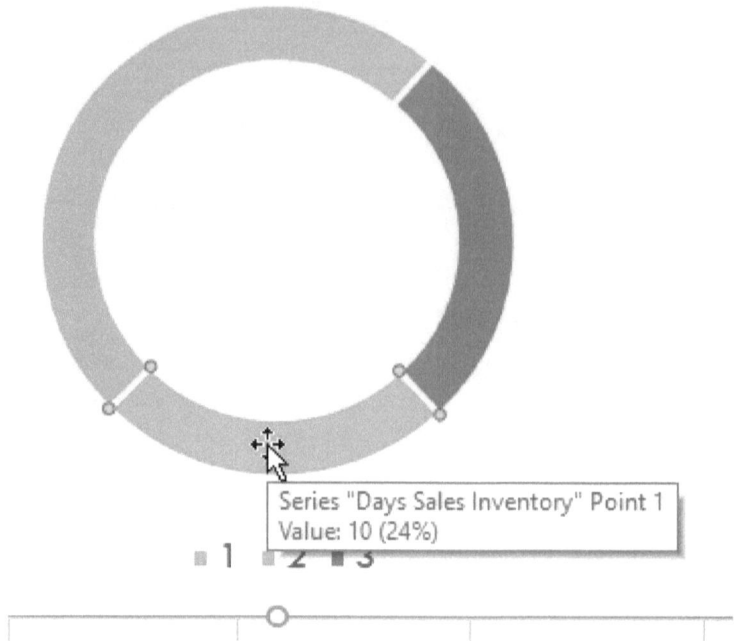

Series "Days Sales Inventory" Point 1
Value: 10 (24%)

6- Go to **Format** tab, and change the **Shape Fill** color to **White, Background 1**.

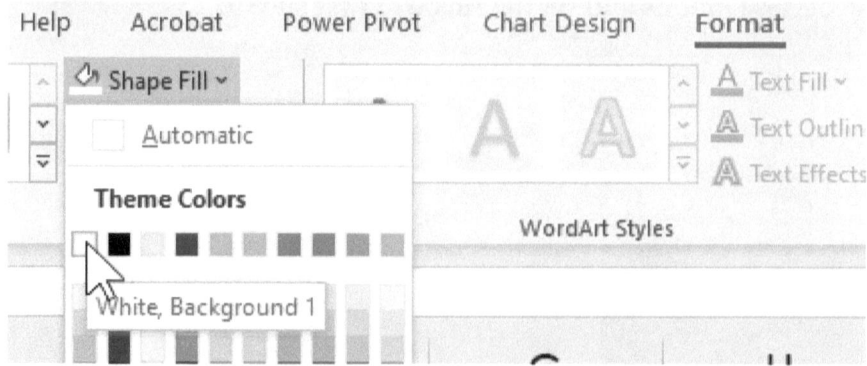

7- Double click the **Point 2** to single select it.

Series "Days Sales Inventory" Point 2
Value: 20 (49%)

8- Go to **Format** tab, and change the **Shape Fill** color to **Dark Blue, Text 2, Darker 25%**.

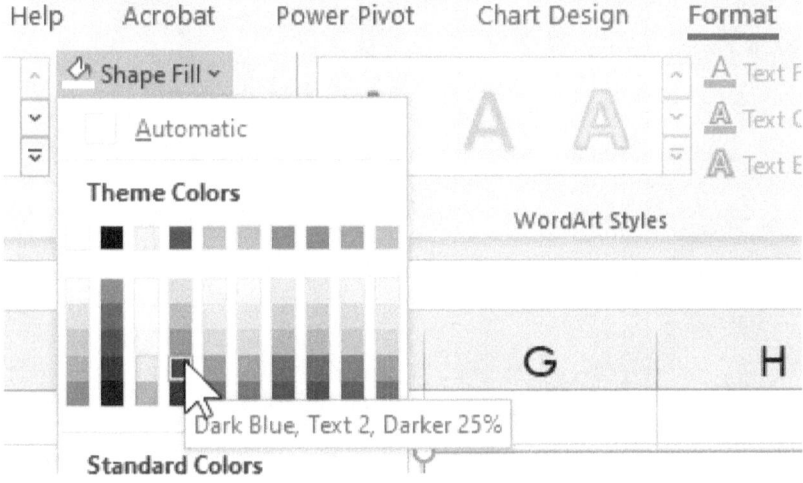

9- Double click the **Point 3** to single select it.

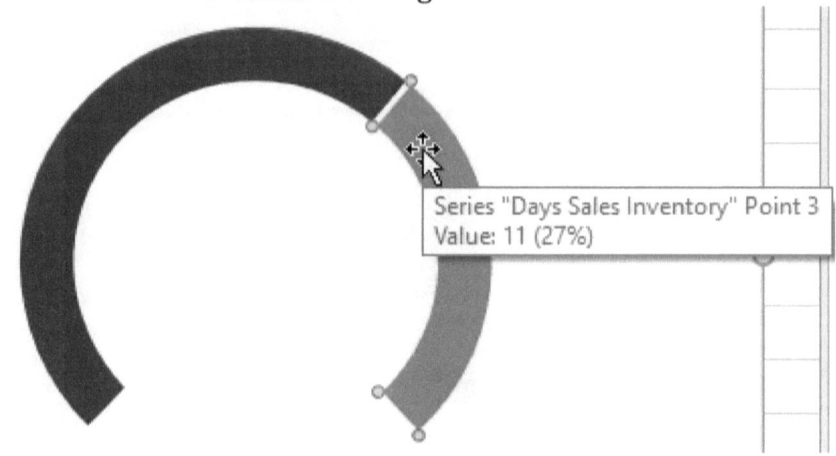

10- Go to **Format** tab, and change the **Shape Fill** color to **White, Background 1, Darker 15%**.

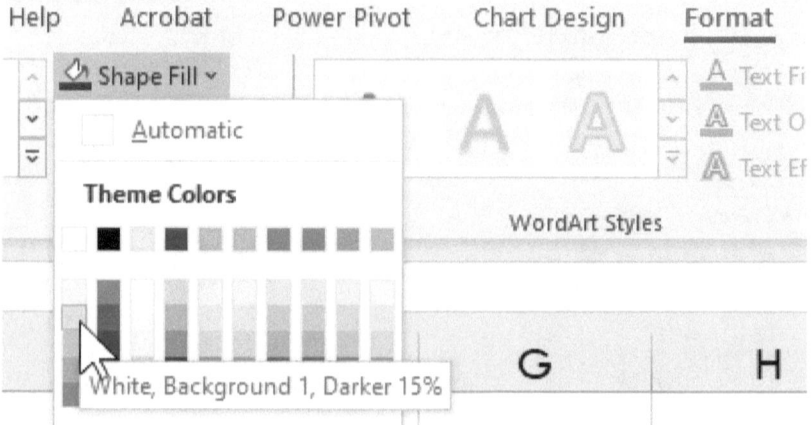

11- With the chart selected click on **Chart Elements** ("+" icon). Then, uncheck **Legend.**

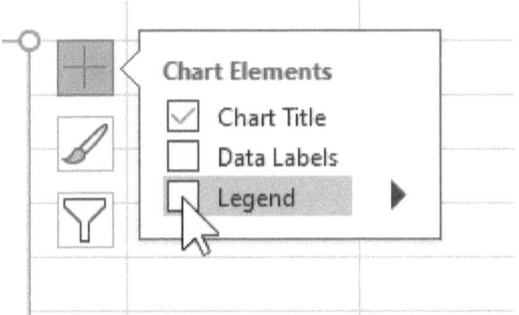

12- Right-click the **Chart Area** and click on **Move Chart**.

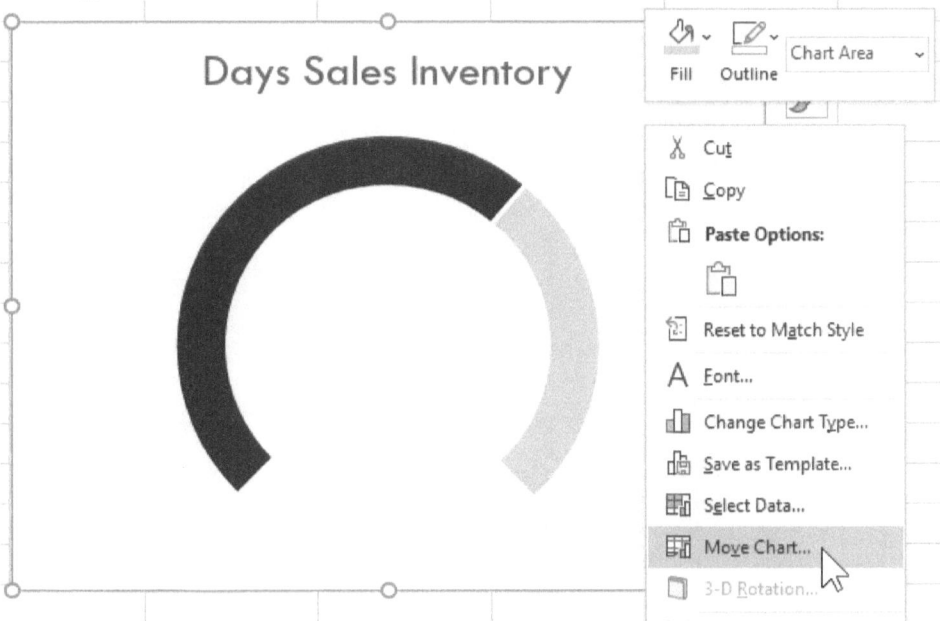

13- Check the option **Object in**, select **Dashboard**, and click **OK**.

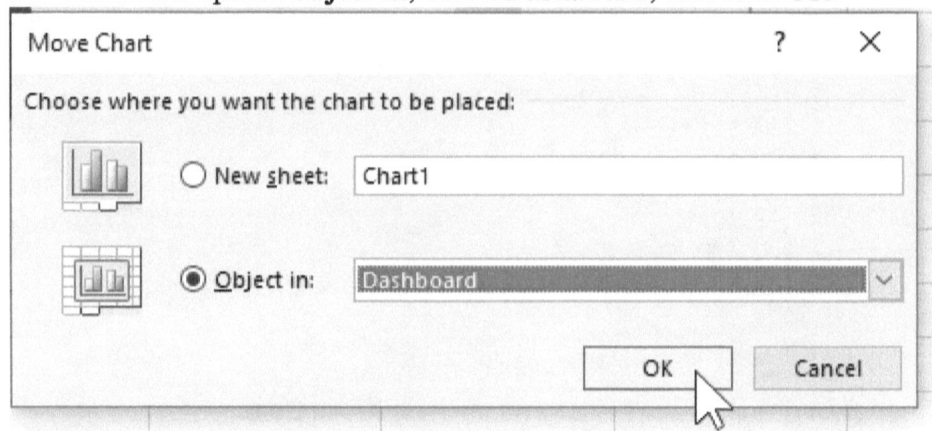

14- Select the chart. Go to **Format** tab and change the **Height** to 6.26 cm, and the **Width** to 6.95 cm.

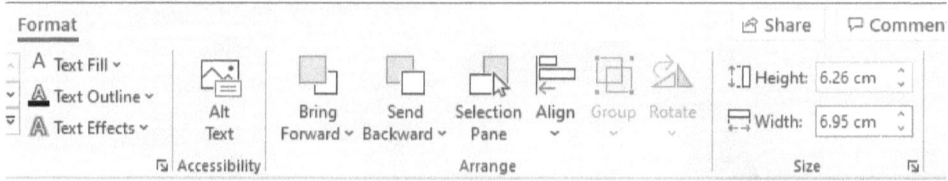

15- Go to **Format** tab, **Shape Outline**, and click on **No Outline**.

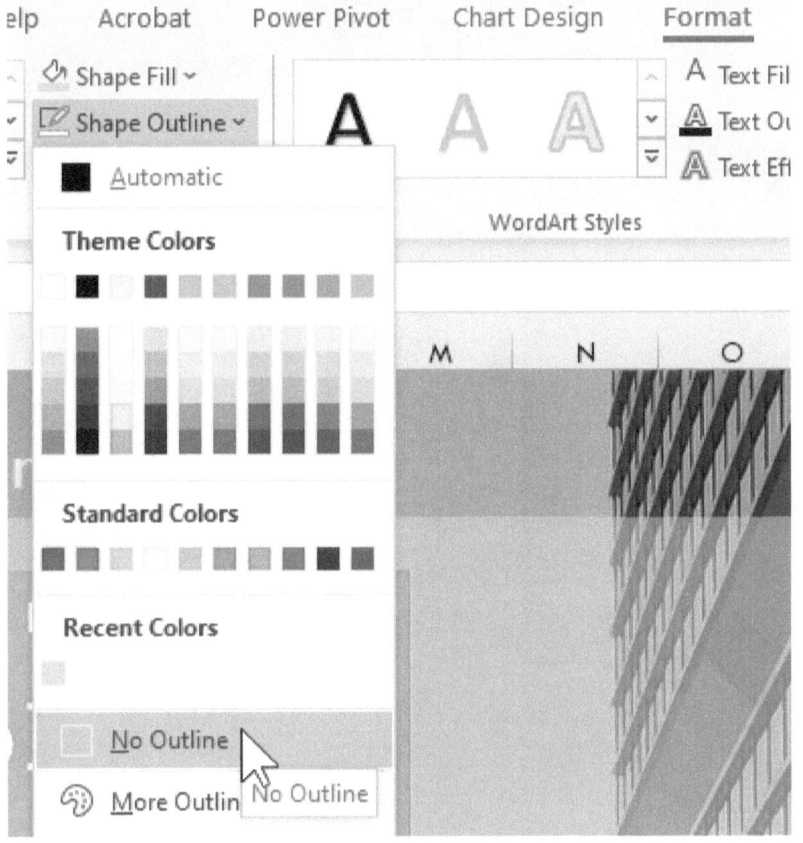

16- Right-click the chart and select **copy**.

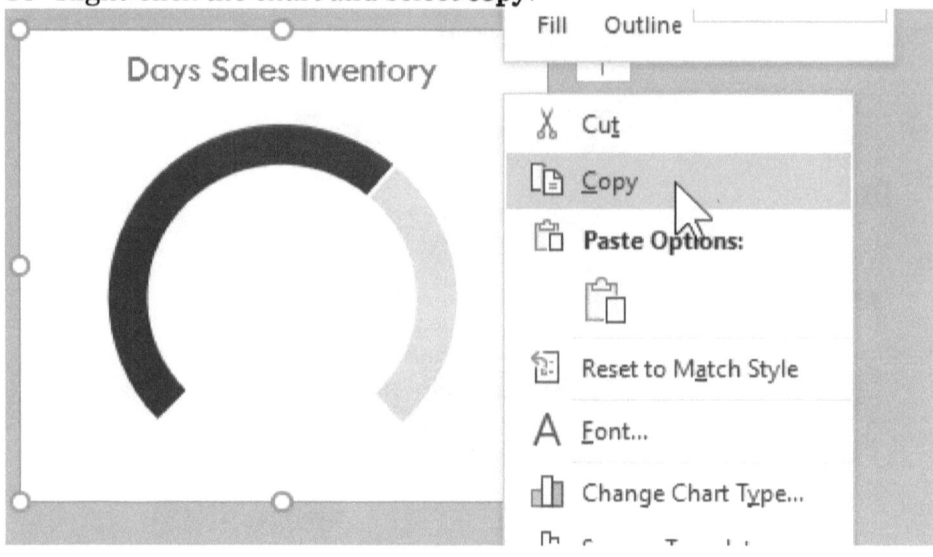

17- Right-click the background and **paste** the new chart.

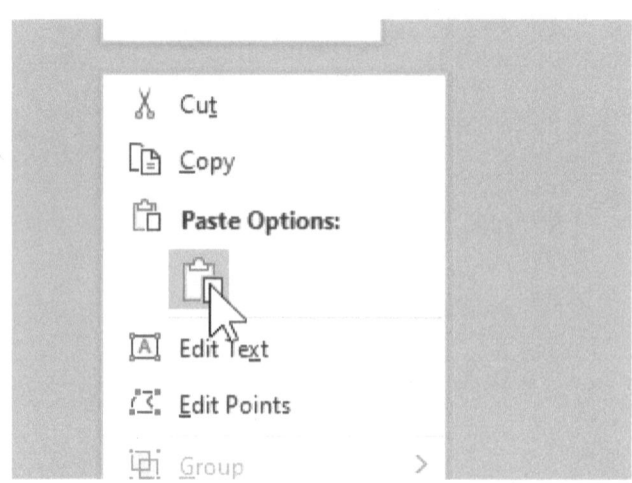

18- With the new chart selected go to **Chart Design** and click on **Select Data**.

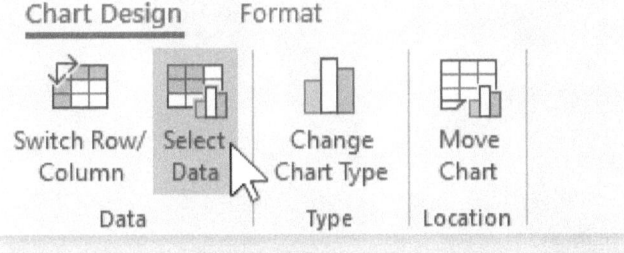

19- Change the **Chart data range** to **=KPIS!$A$3:$D$3**. Then, click **OK**.

	A	B	C	D	E
1		White	Data	Gap	
2	Days Sales Inventory	10	20	11	41
3	Days Sales Outstanding	10	12	19	41
4	Days Payable Outstanding	10	26	5	41
5	Equity Ratio	61.70%			

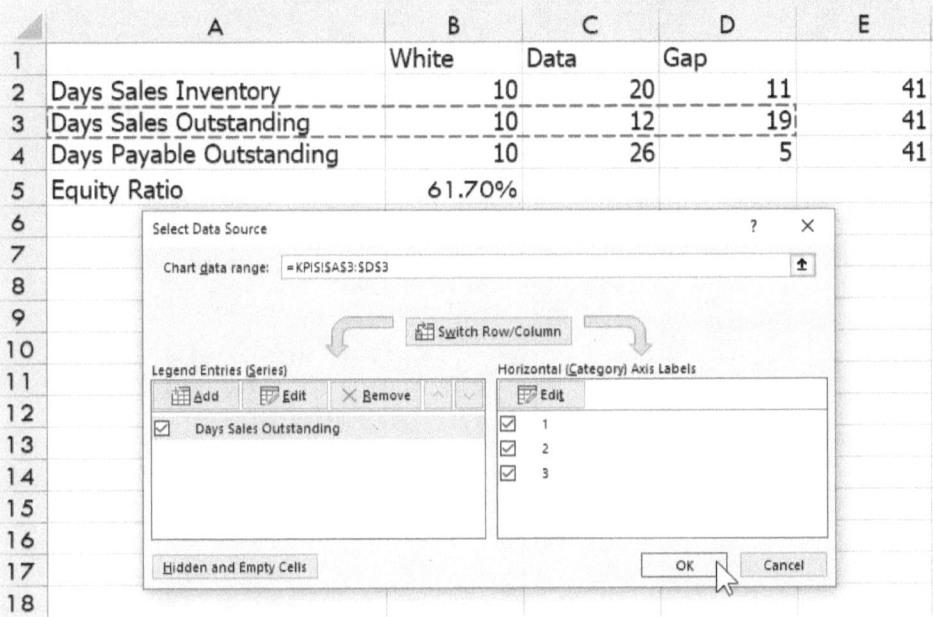

20- Double click the **Point 1** to single select it. Then,Go to **Format** tab, and change the **Shape Fill** color to **White, Background 1**.

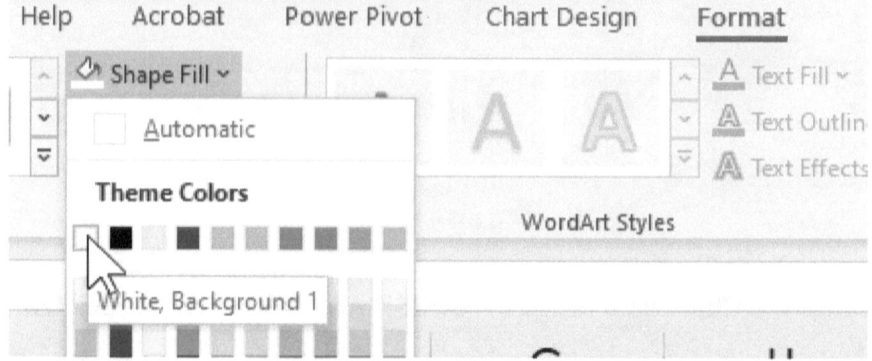

21- Double click the **Point 3** to single select it. Then, go to **Format** tab, and change the **Shape Fill** color to **White, Background 1, Darker 15%**.

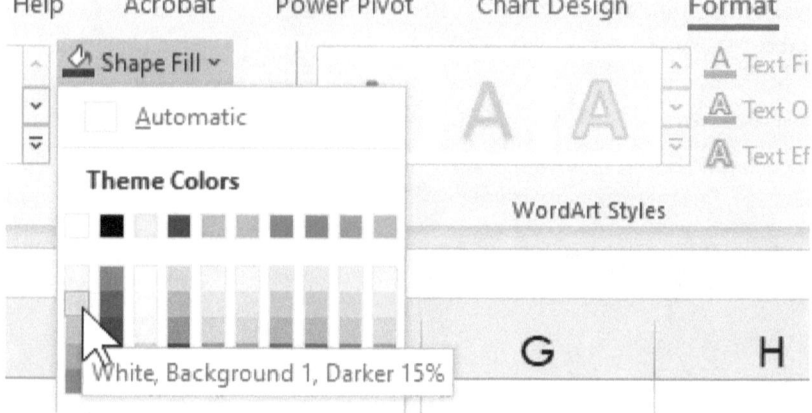

22- Double click the **Point 2** to single select it. Then, Go to **Format** tab, and change the **Shape Fill** color to **Red, Accent 3, Darker 25%.**

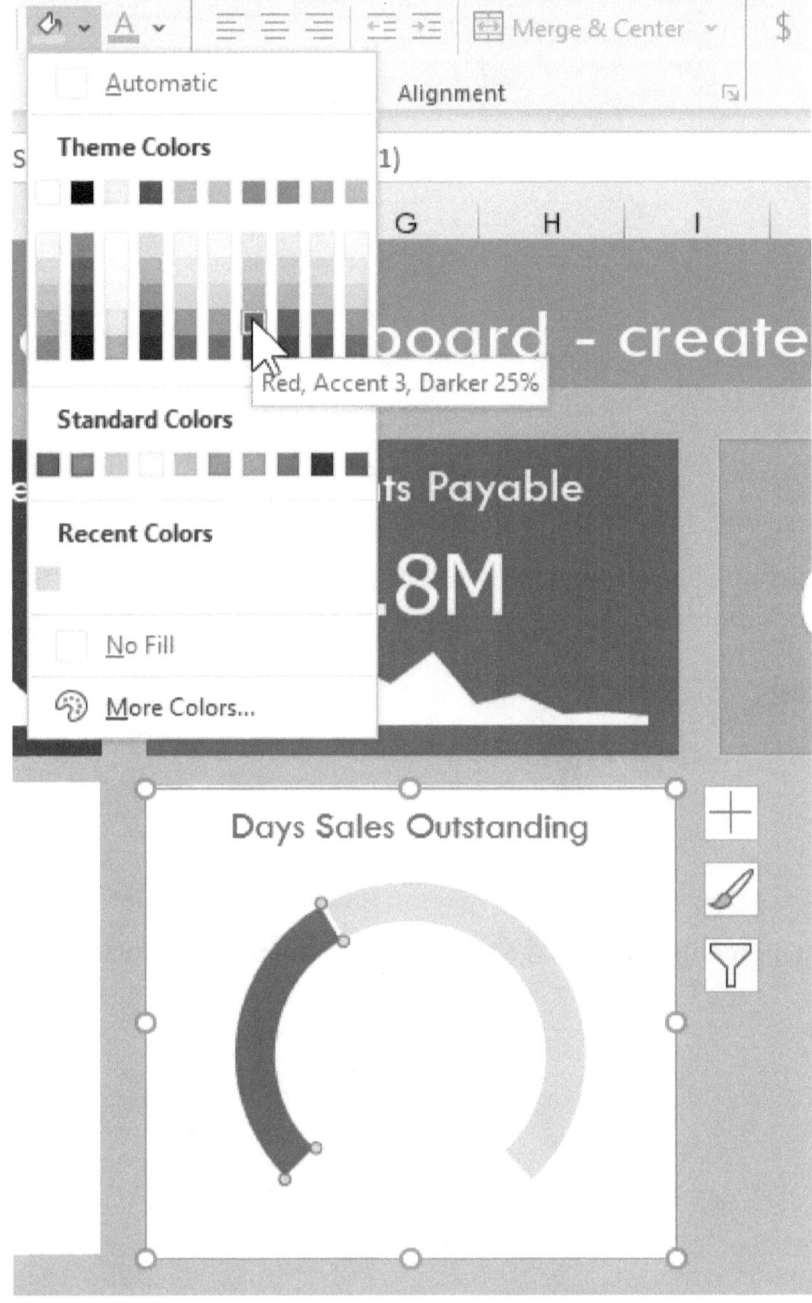

23- Right-click the chart and select **copy**.

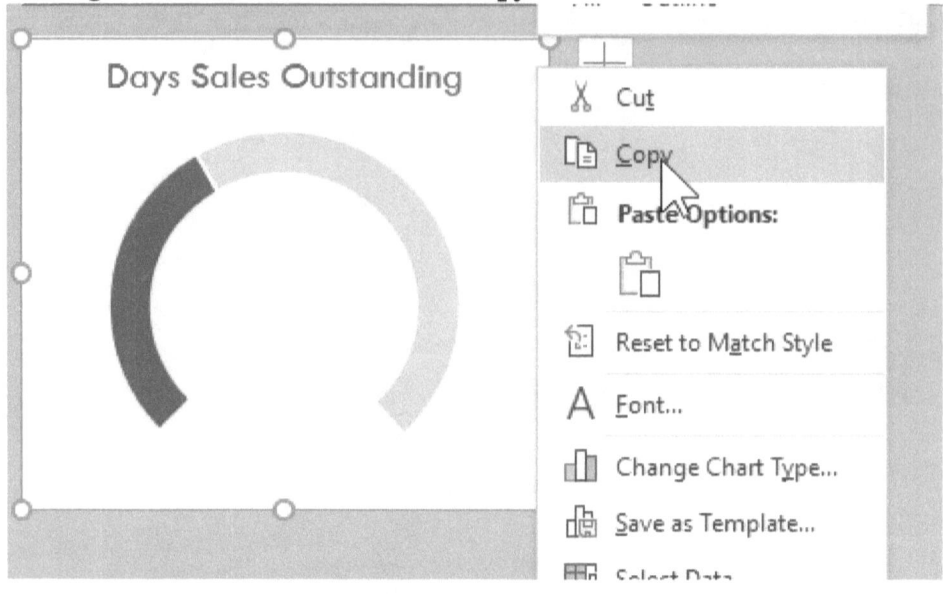

24- Right-click the background and **paste** the new chart.

25- With the new chart selected go to **Chart Design** and click on **Select Data**.

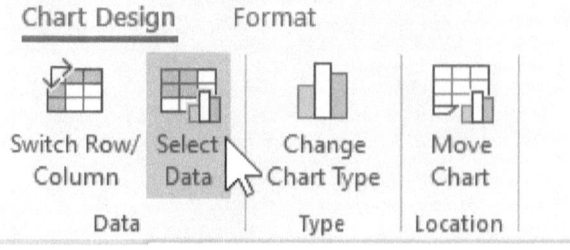

26- Change the **Chart data range** to **=KPIS!$A$4:$D$4**. Then, click **OK**.

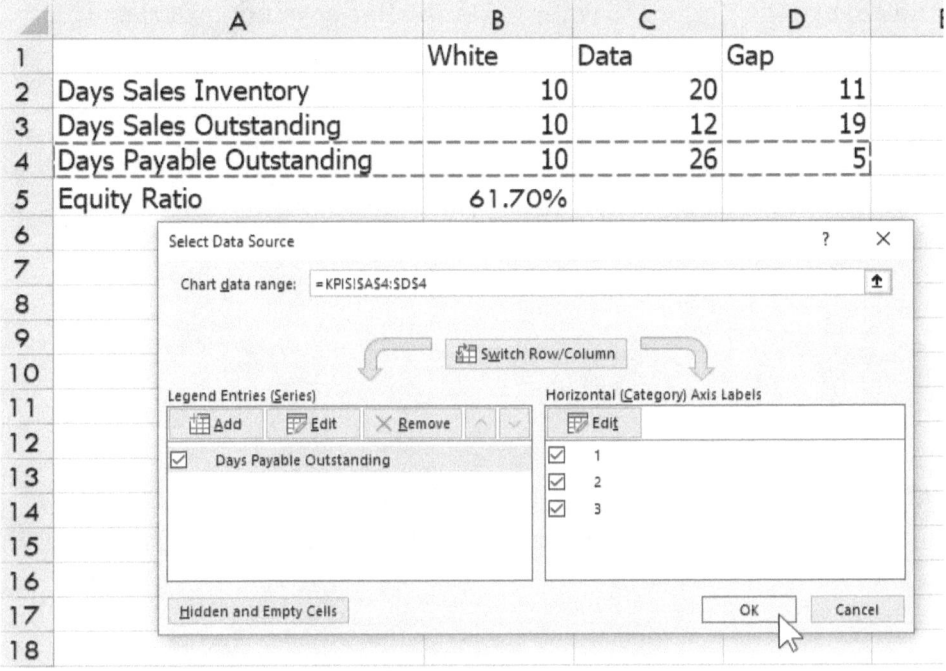

	A	B	C	D	
1		White	Data	Gap	
2	Days Sales Inventory	10	20	11	
3	Days Sales Outstanding	10	12	19	
4	Days Payable Outstanding	10	26	5	
5	Equity Ratio	61.70%			

Select Data Source

Chart data range: =KPIS!$A$4:$D$4

Switch Row/Column

Legend Entries (Series)

Add   Edit   Remove

☑ Days Payable Outstanding

Horizontal (Category) Axis Labels

Edit

☑ 1
☑ 2
☑ 3

Hidden and Empty Cells   OK   Cancel

27- Double click the **Point 1** to single select it. Then, go to **Format** tab, and change the **Shape Fill** color to **White, Background 1**.

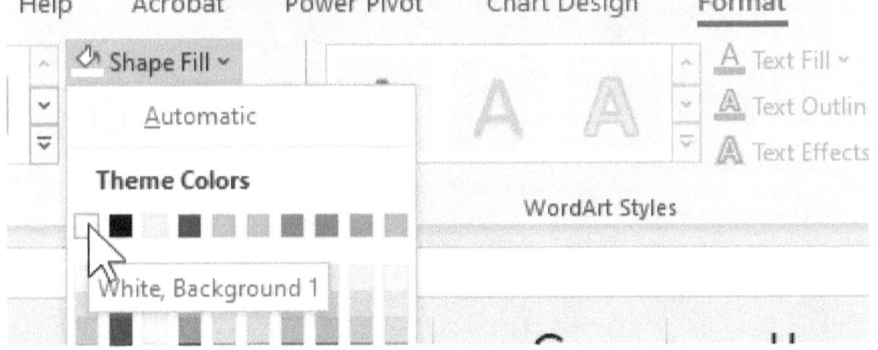

Help   Acrobat   Power Pivot   Chart Design   Format

Shape Fill ˅

Automatic

Theme Colors

White, Background 1

A Text Fill ˅
A Text Outlin
A Text Effects

WordArt Styles

28- Double click the **Point 3** to single select it. Then, go to **Format** tab, and change the **Shape Fill** color to **White, Background 1, Darker 15%**.

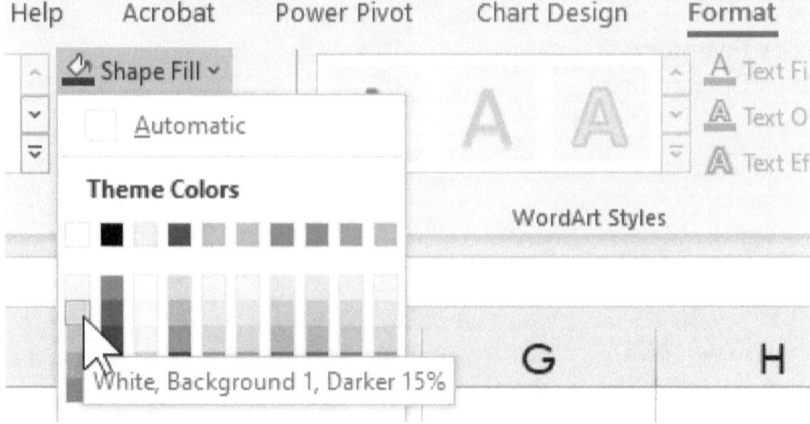

29- Double click the **Point 2** to single select it. Then, Go to **Format** tab, and change the **Shape Fill** color to **Sky Blue, Background 2, Darker 50%**.

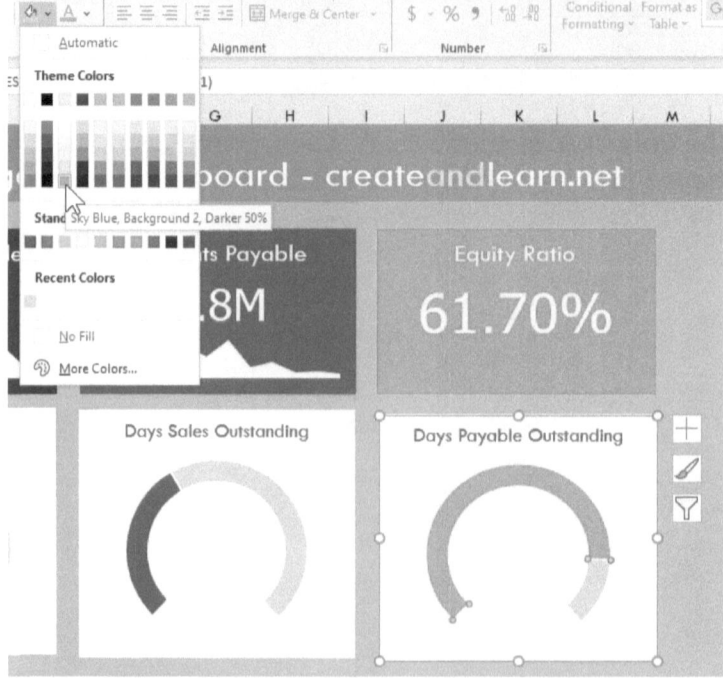

30- Move the charts to organize them like the image below. Then, hold **ctrl** and click to select the three doughnut charts

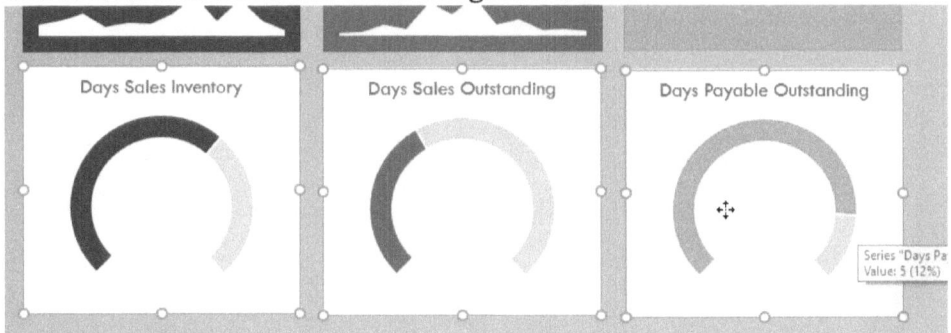

31- Go **Shape Format**, click on **Align** and choose the alignment that makes sense to your need, in this example was used **Align Top**.

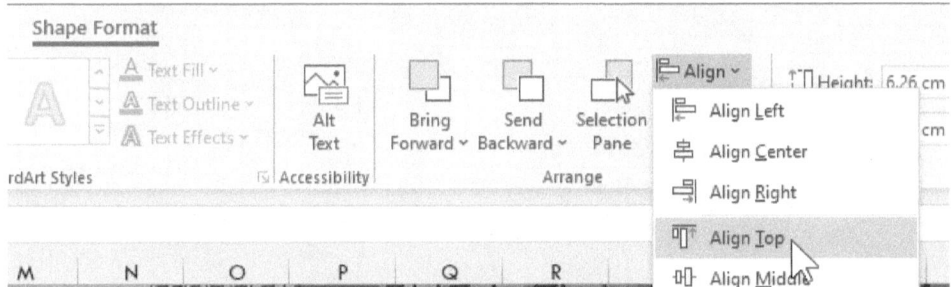

32- To create the internal numbers, go to **Insert** tab and add a new text box.

33- With the text box selected, type "=" in the formula bar, to start creating a link to a cell.

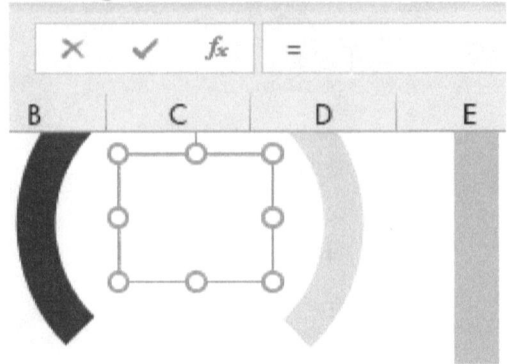

34- Go to **KPIS** sheet and click on cell **C2**, this will add cell address to the text box formula. Then, press **Enter**.

	A	B	C	
1		White	Data	
2	Days Sales Inventory	10	⊕ 20	
3	Days Sales Outstanding	10	12	
4	Days Payable Outstanding	10	26	
5	Equity Ratio	61.70%		

35- Move the text box over of the first doughnut.

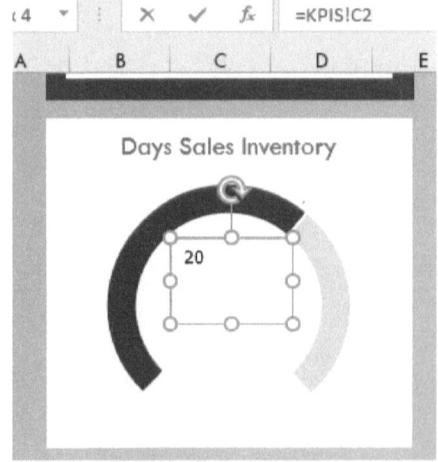

36- With the text box selected, go to **Shape Format** tab, **Shape Outline**, and click on **No Outline**.

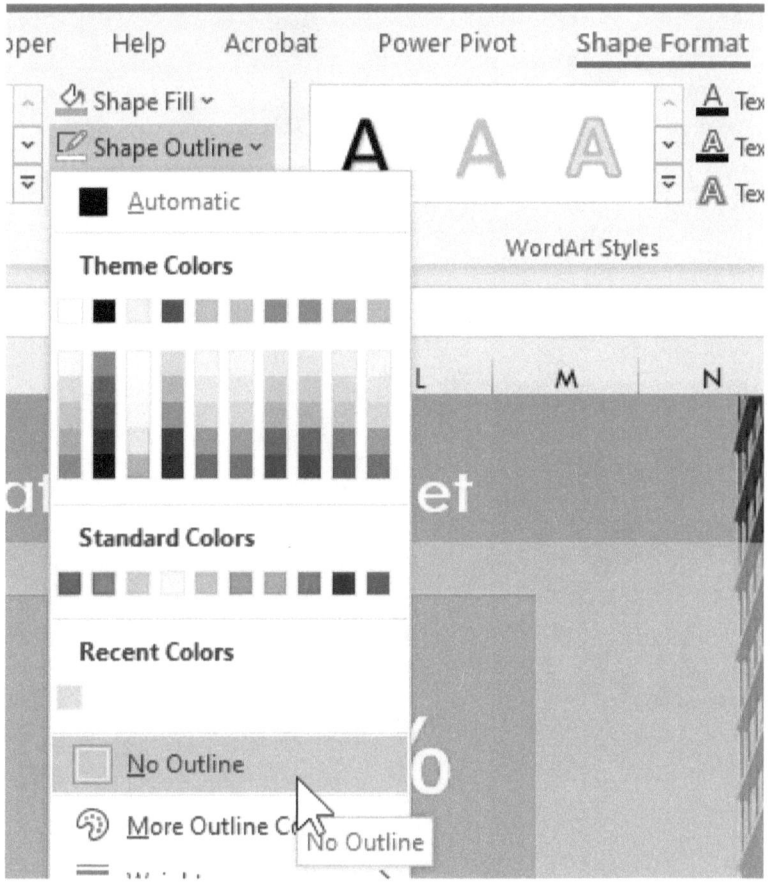

37- With the text box selected go to **Home** tab, and change the font to **Tahoma**, size **44**, font color **Black, Text 1, Lighter 25%** and **Center** alignment.

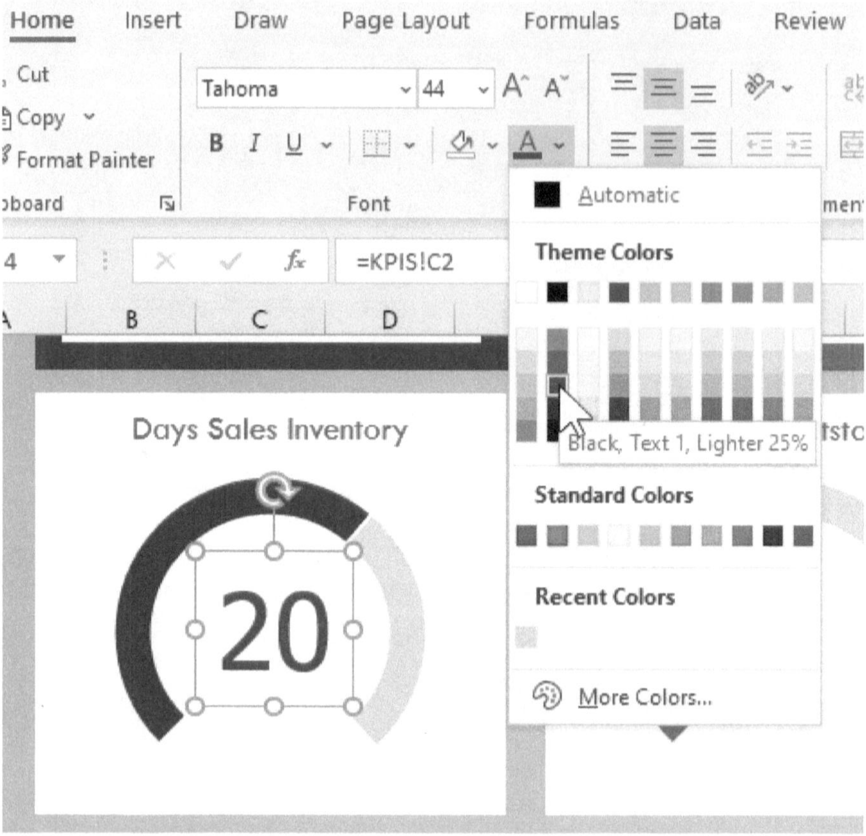

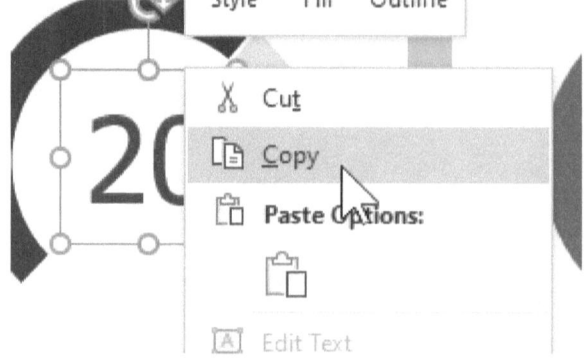

38- Right-click the text box and select **Copy**.

39- Paste it **two** times and move the text boxes to look like the image below.

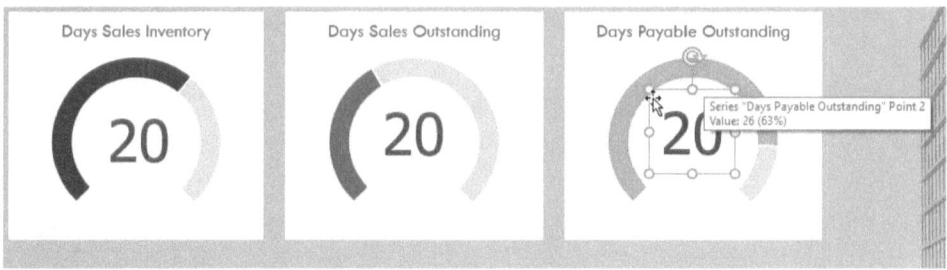

40- On the **Days Sales Outstanding** text box, change the formula to **=KPIS!C3**.

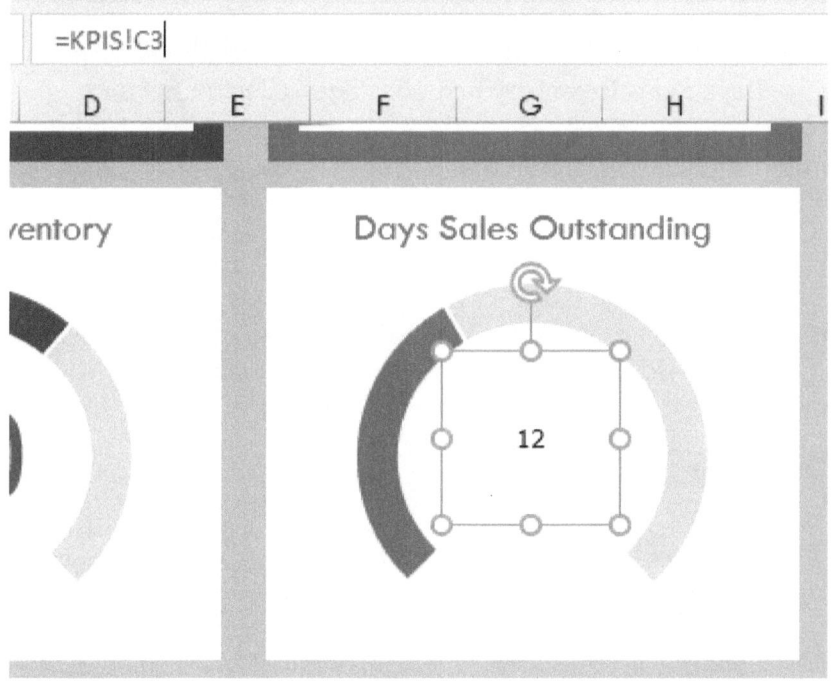

41- On the **Days Payable Outstanding** text box, change the formula to **=KPIS!C4**.

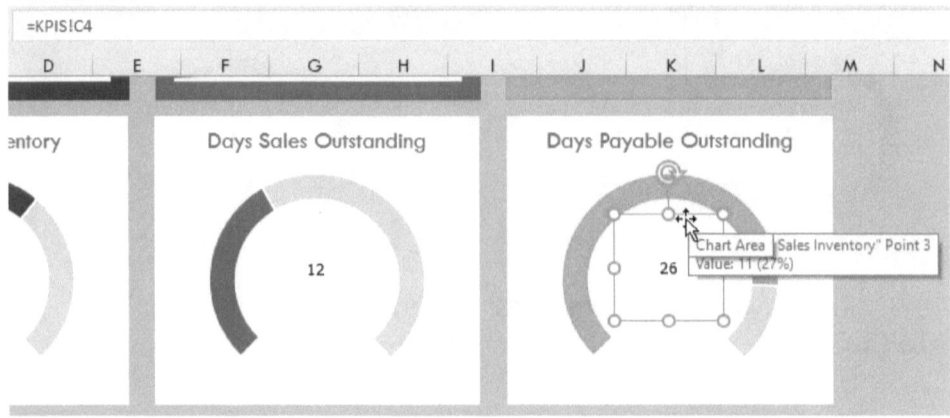

42- Select the **Days Sales Inventory** text box. Then click on **Format Painter** to copy the text box style.

43- Click on both unformatted text boxes to paste the style.

44- Hold **ctrl** and click to select the three text boxes

45- Then, go **Shape Format**, click on **Align** and choose the alignment that makes sense to your need, in this example was used **Align Middle**.

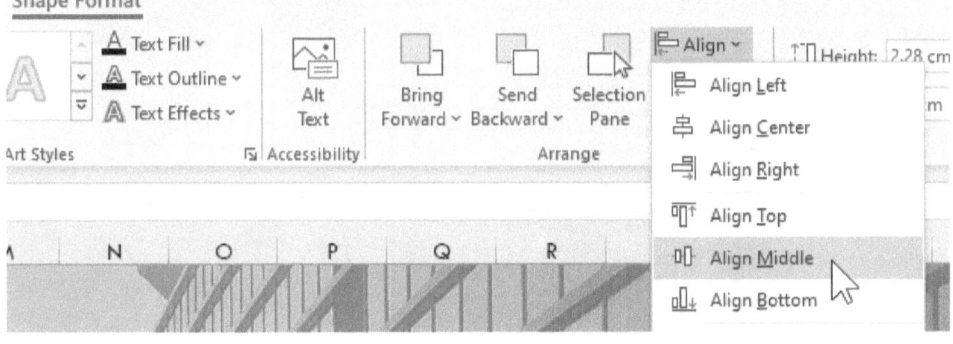

46- Drag and drop the objects to have a Dashboard like the image below.

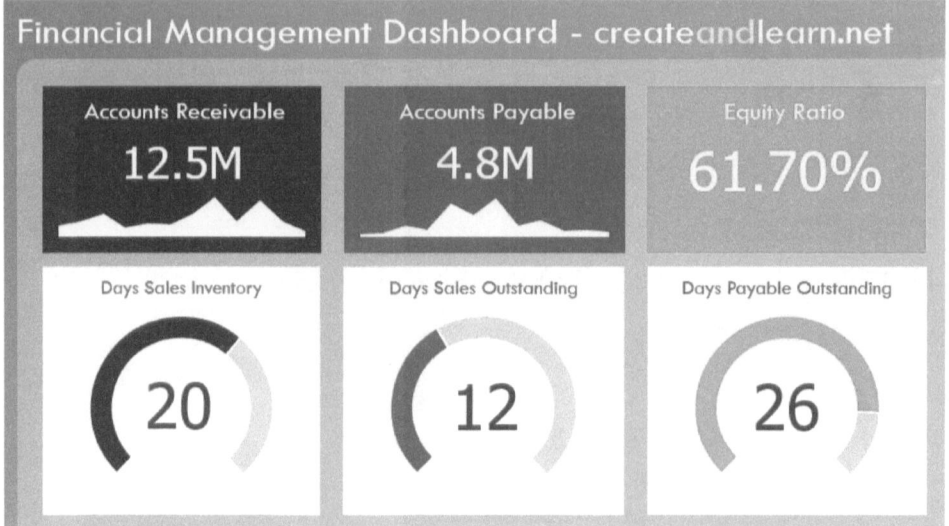

9.Using Column Chart to show comparisons

1- Go to **Accounts** sheet.

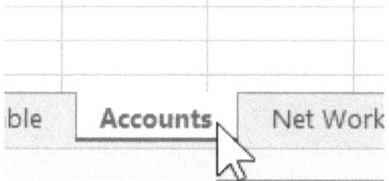

2- Select the range **A1:C6**. Then, Go to **Insert** tab, **Charts** and select the **Clustered Column**.

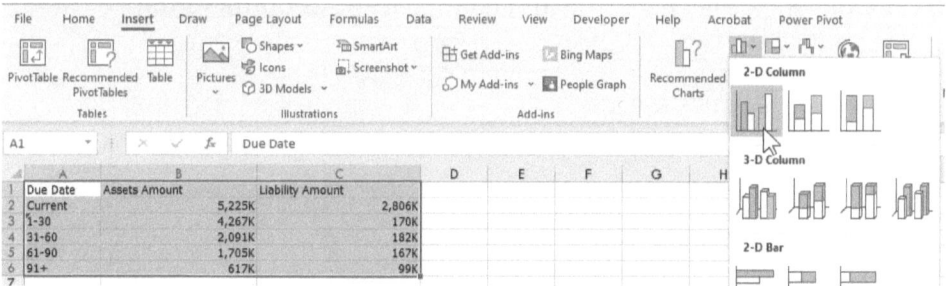

3- With the chart selected click on **Chart Elements** ("+" icon). Then, uncheck **Gridlines**.

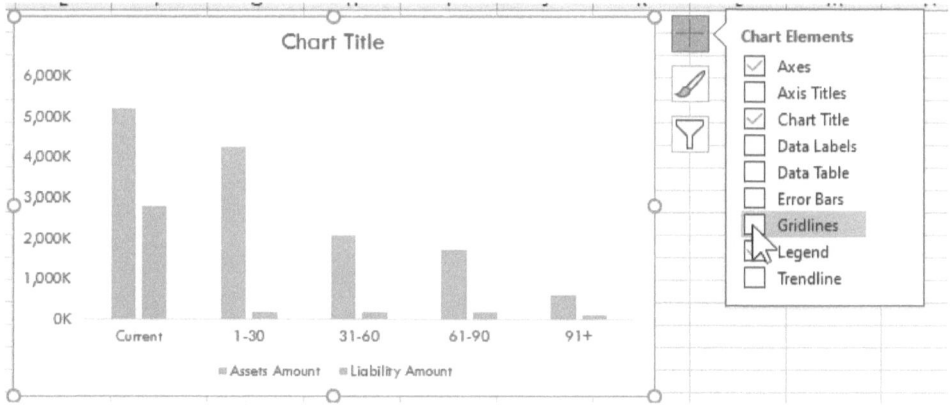

4- Go to **Axes** and uncheck **Primary Vertical**.

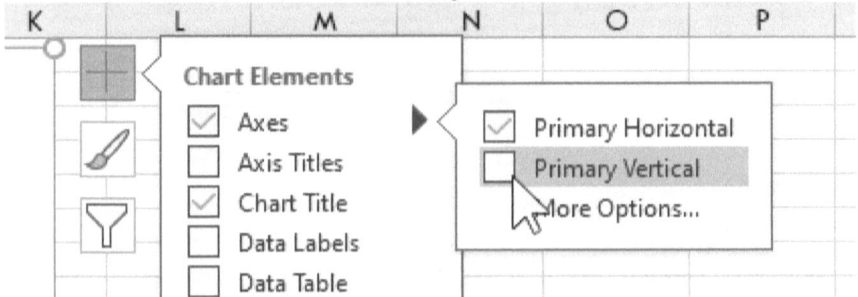

5- Double click the chart title and change it to **Accounts Aging**.

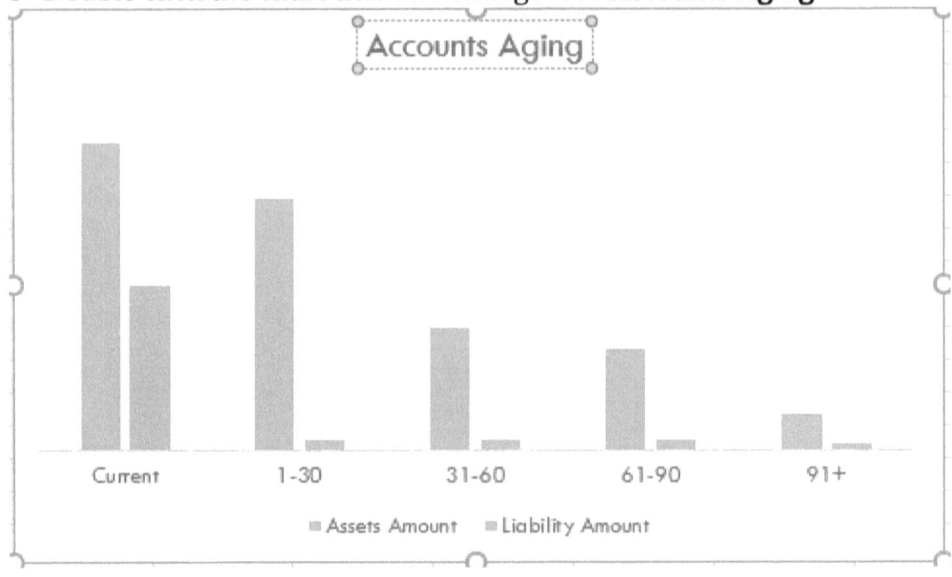

6- Click on the first **Assets Amount** bar to select the series.

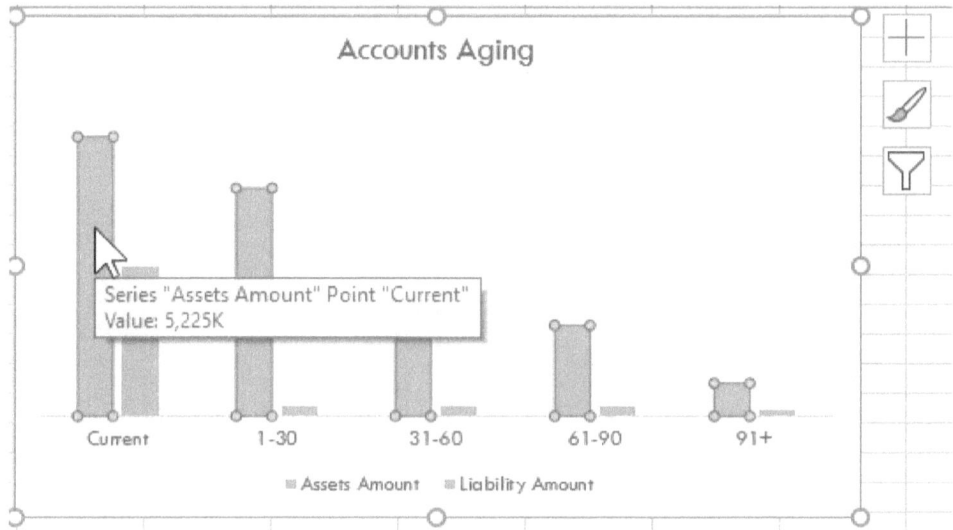

7- Go to **Home** tab, and change the **Fill** color to **Dark Blue, Text 2, Darker 25%**.

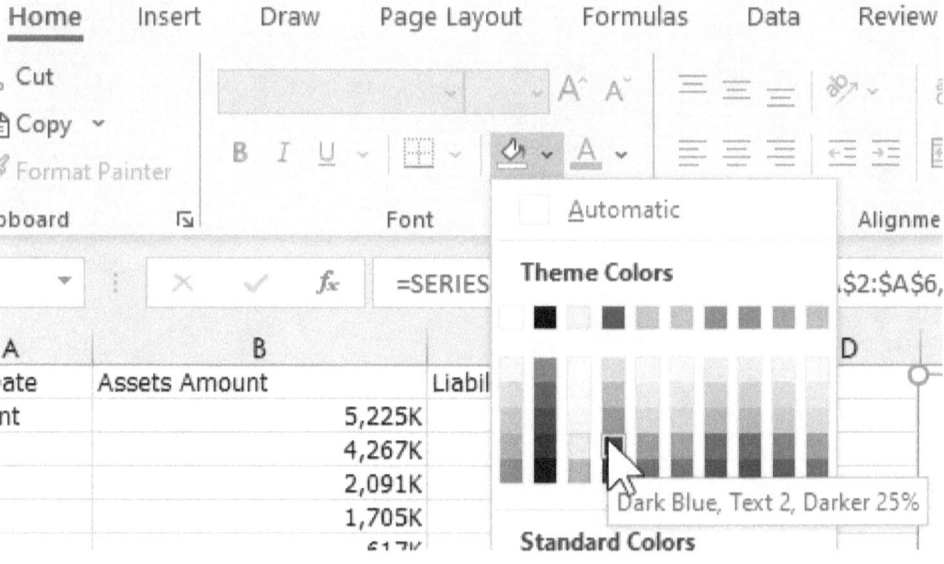

8- Click on the first **Liability Amount** bar to select the series.

9- Go to **Home** tab, and change the **Fill** color to **White, Background 1, Darker 35%**.

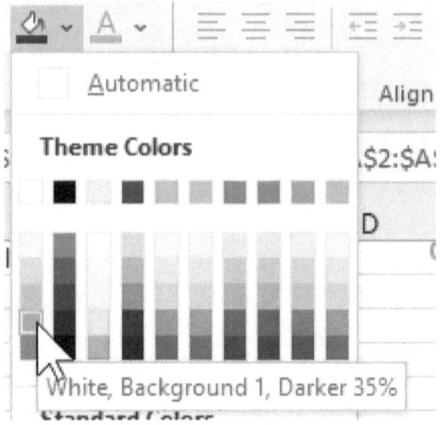

10- With the chart selected click on **Chart Elements** ("+" icon). Then, check **Data Labels**.

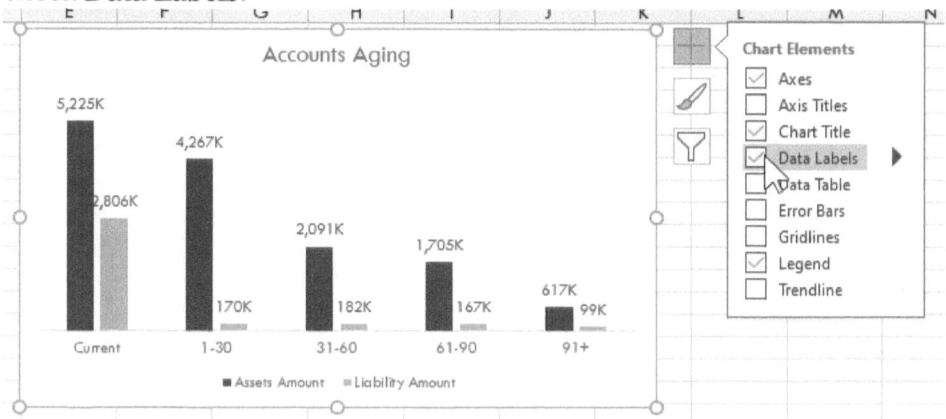

11- Right-click the **Chart Area** and click on **Move Chart**.

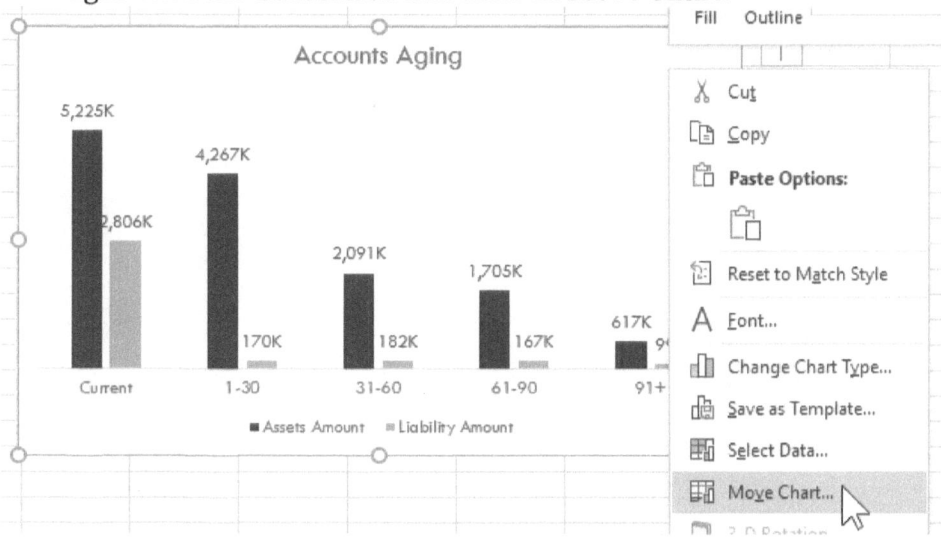

12- Check the option **Object in**, select **Dashboard**, and click OK.

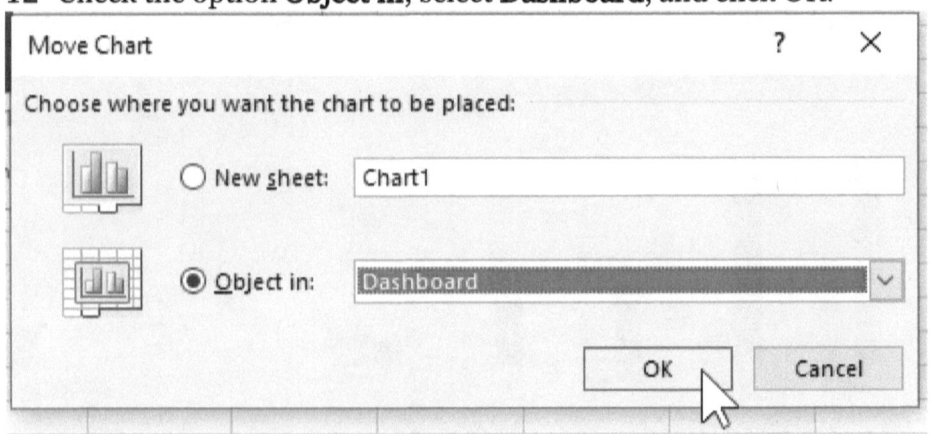

13- Select the chart. Go to **Format** tab and change the **Height** to 9.63 cm, and the **Width** to 22.03 cm.

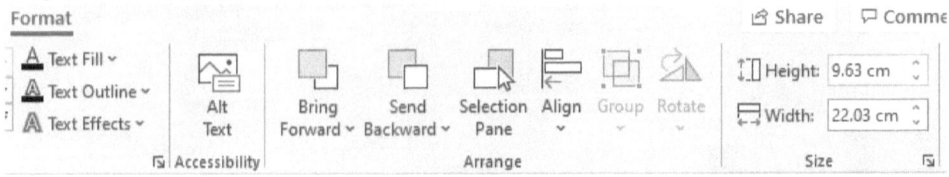

14- Go to **Format** tab, **Shape Outline,** and click on **No Outline**.

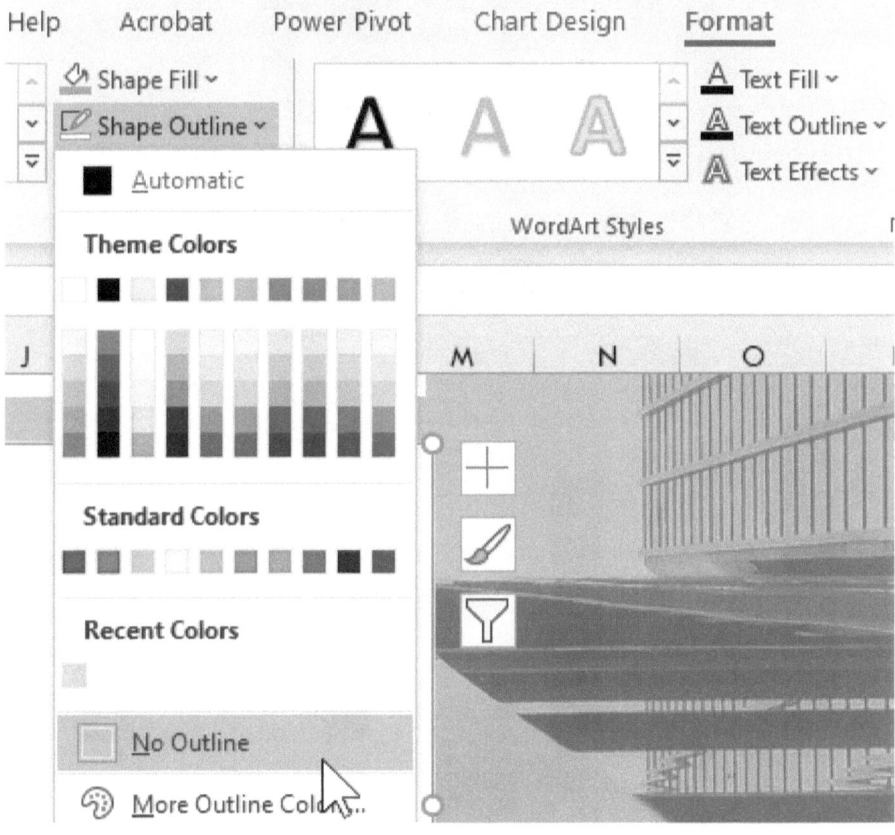

15- Select the **legend**. Go to **Home** tab and change the text size to **11**.

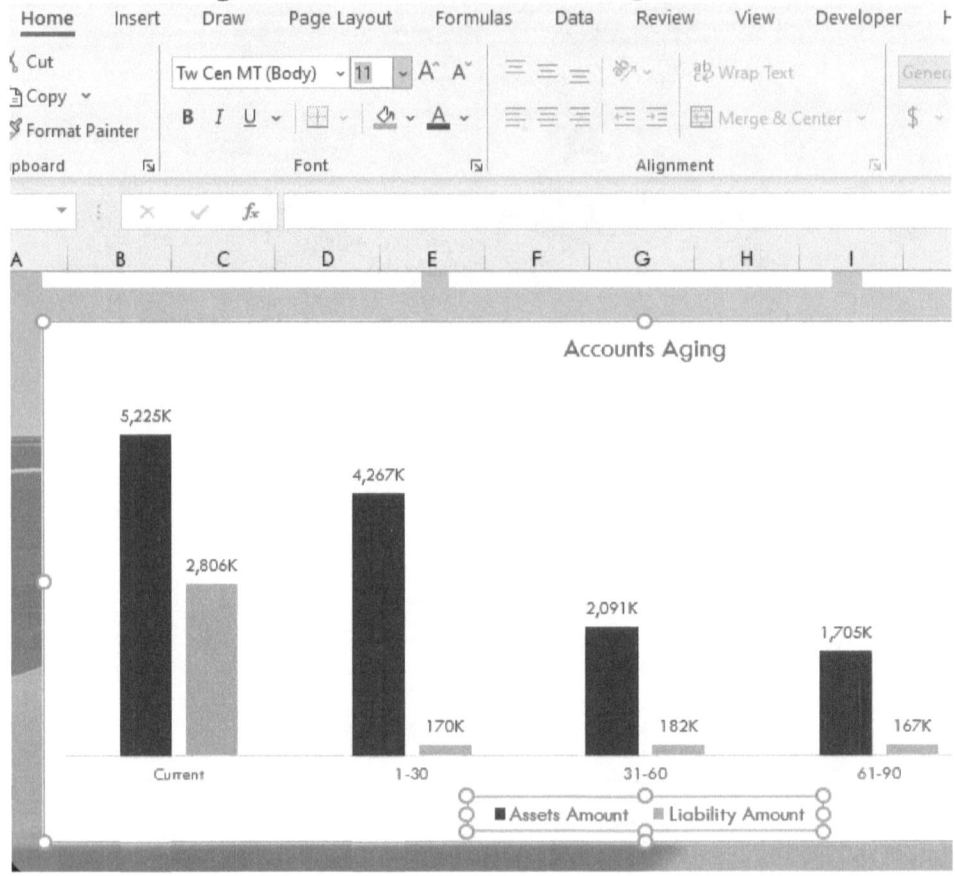

16- Select the **Data labels** and change the text size to **11**.

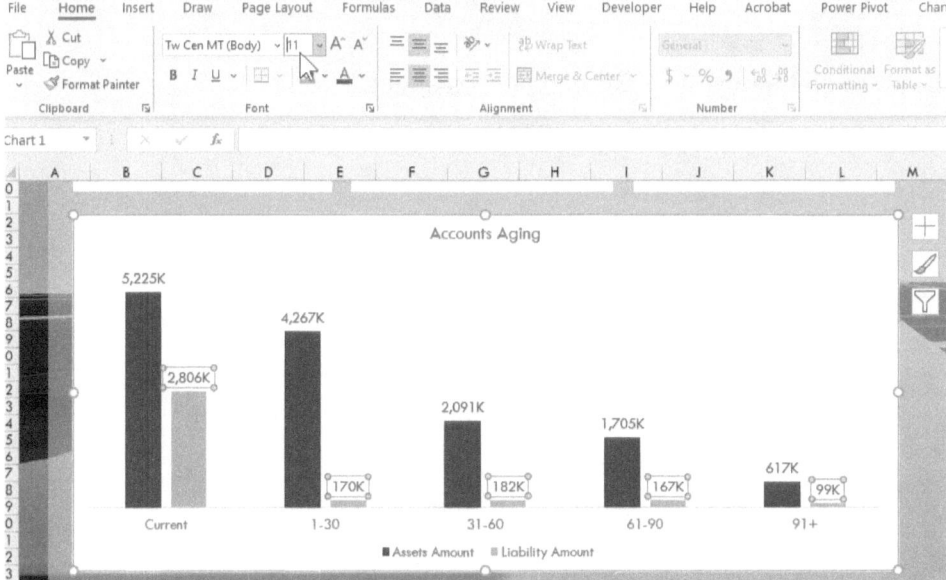

17- Drag and drop the objects to have a Dashboard like the image below.

10.Using Line Chart to show Evolution through time

1- Go to Net Working Capital vs Gross sheet.

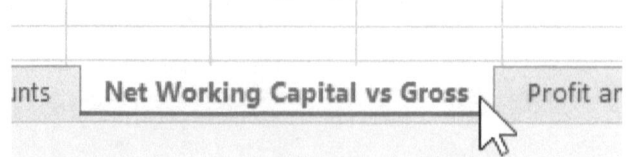

2- Select the range A1:C13. Then, go to Insert tab, Charts and select the Line chart.

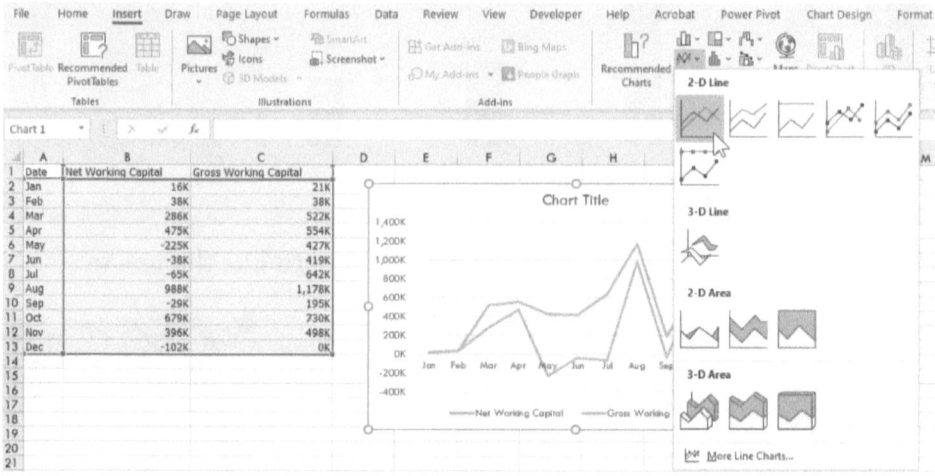

3- Change the chart title to **Net Working Capital vs. Gross Working Capital**.

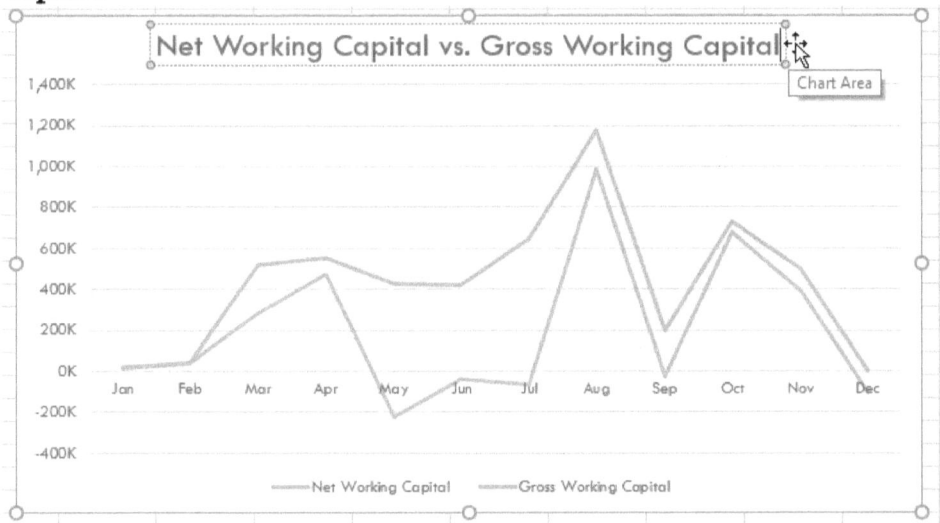

4- Right-click the **Gross Working Capital** line and click on **Format Data Series**.

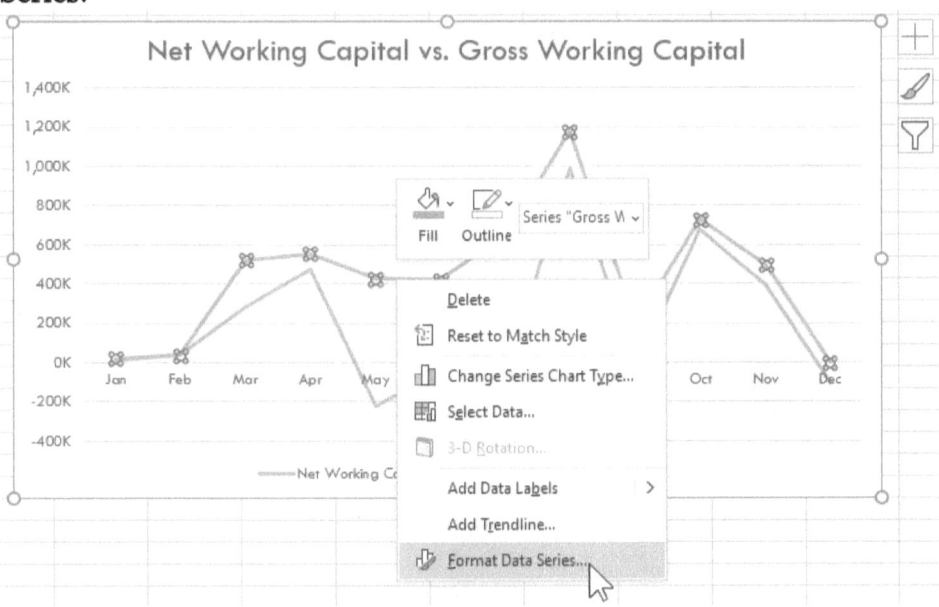

5- Go to **Fill & Line** and change the **Color** to **Dark Blue, Text 2, Darker 25%**.

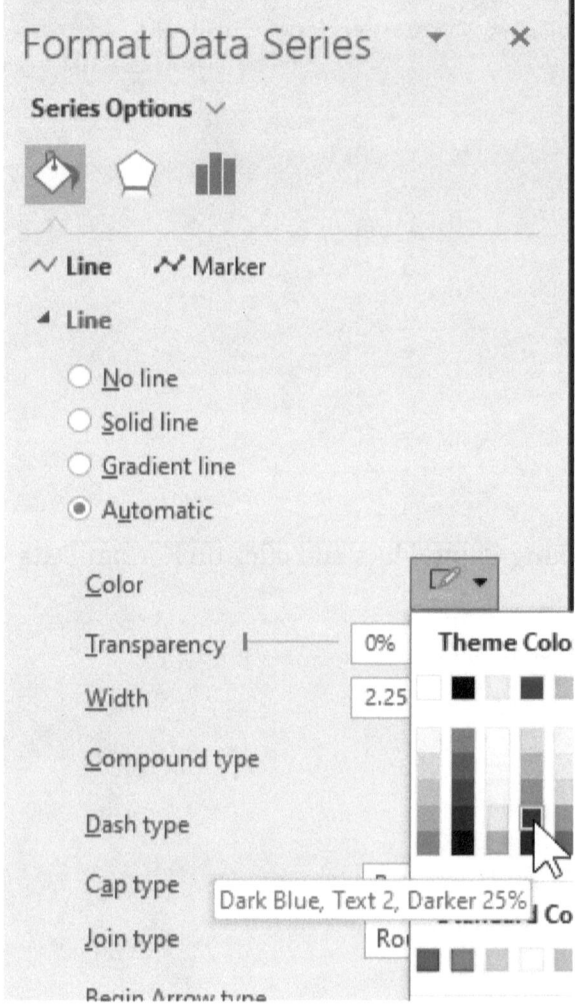

6- Change the **width** to 4 pt, and check the box **Smoothed line**.

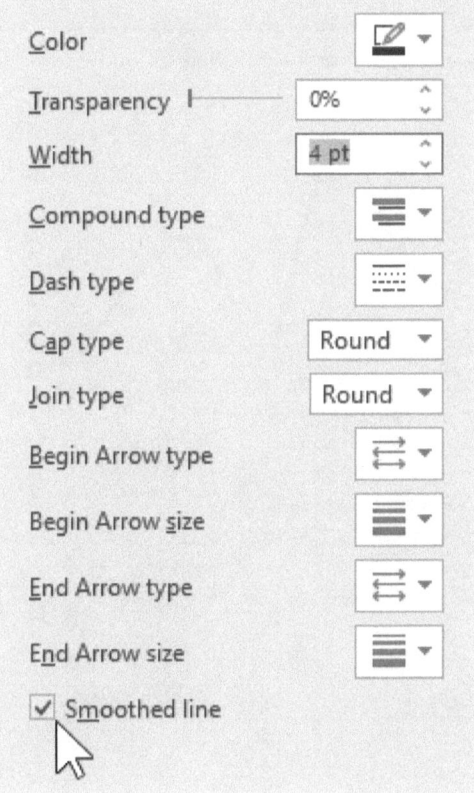

7- Right-click the **Net Working Capital** line and click on **Format Data Series**.

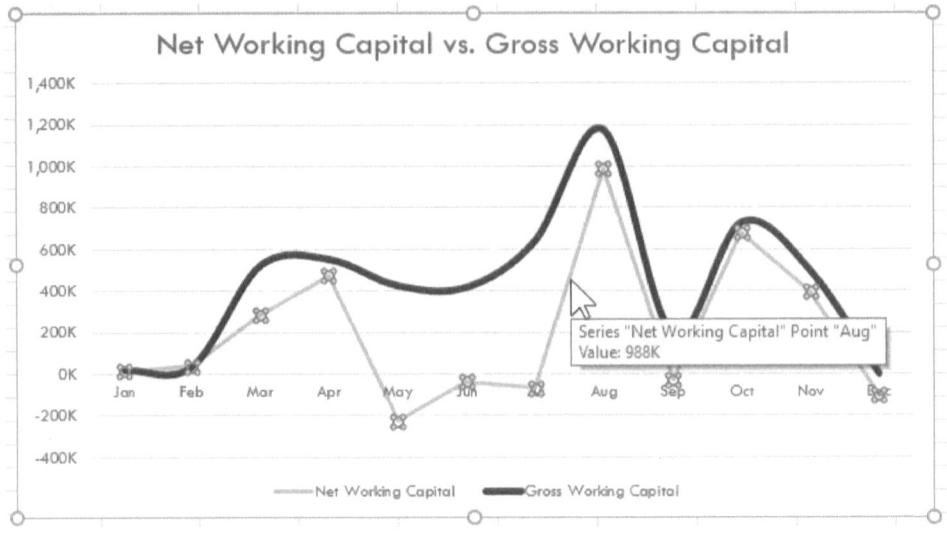

8- Change the **width** to 4 pt, and check the box **Smoothed line**. Then, Change the **Color** to **Sky Blue, Background 2, Darker 50%**

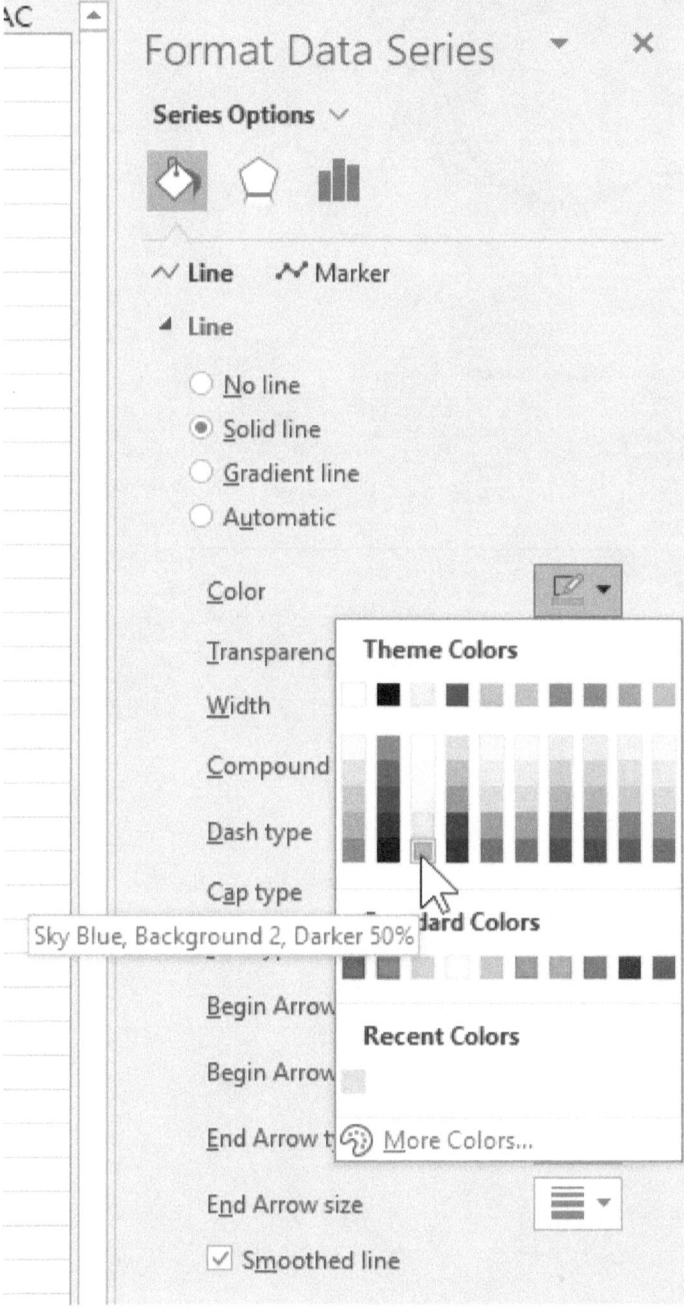

9- Right click the vertical axis and select **Format Axis**.

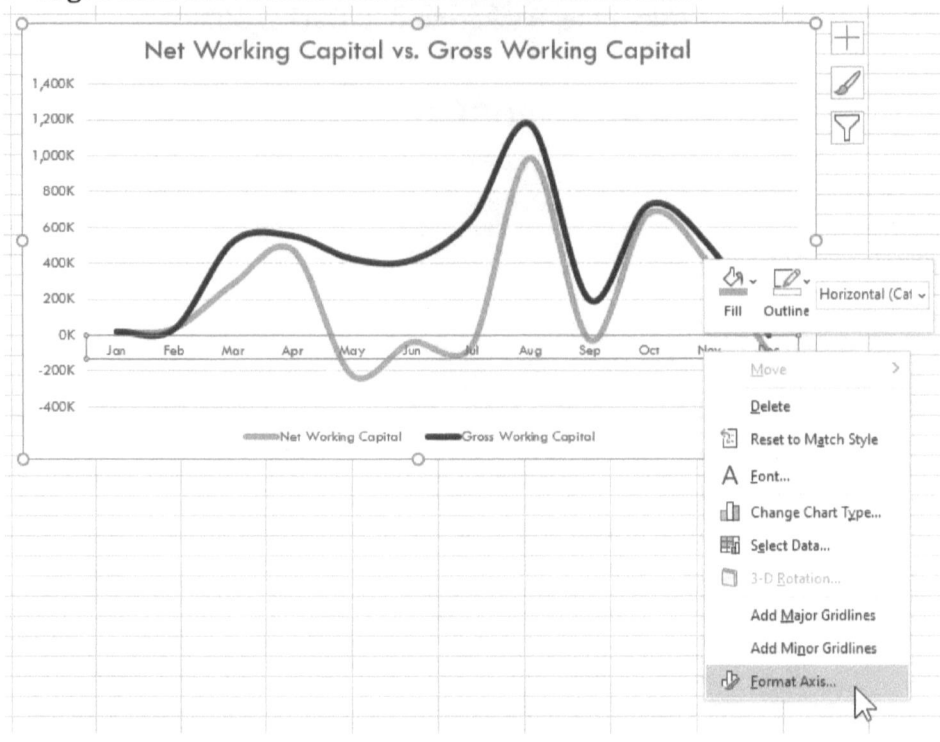

10- On **Axis Options** change the **Label Position** to **Low**.

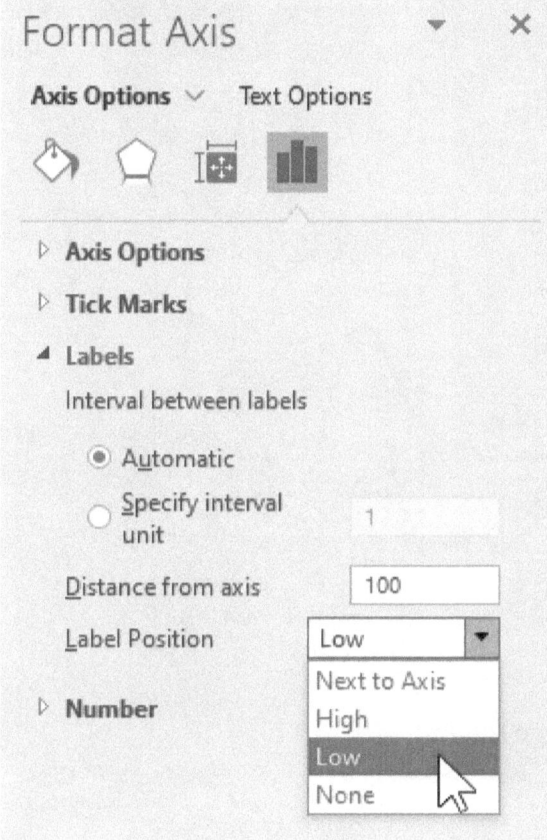

11- Change the Vertical and Horizontal Axis' **font size** to 12.

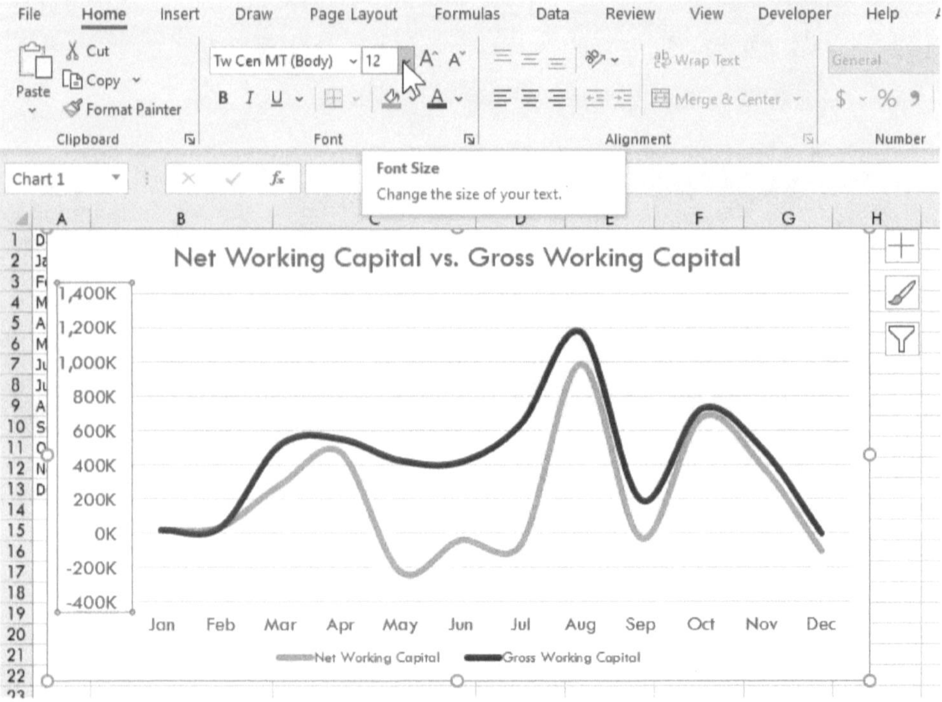

File	Home	Insert	Draw	Page Layout	Formulas	Data	Review	View	Developer	Help

Paste — Cut, Copy, Format Painter | Clipboard

Tw Cen MT (Body) ⌄ | 12 | A˄ A˅ | B I U ⌄ | ⊞ ⌄ | A ⌄ | Font

Font Size
Change the size of your text.

≡ ≡ ≡ | ab Wrap Text | General
≡ ≡ ≡ | Merge & Center ⌄ | $ ⌄ % ⟩
Alignment | Number

Chart 1 | fx

Net Working Capital vs. Gross Working Capital

1,400K
1,200K
1,000K
800K
600K
400K
200K
0K
-200K
-400K

Jan Feb Mar Apr May Jun Jul Aug Sep Oct Nov Dec

Net Working Capital   Gross Working Capital

12- Select the legend and change the **font size** to 11.

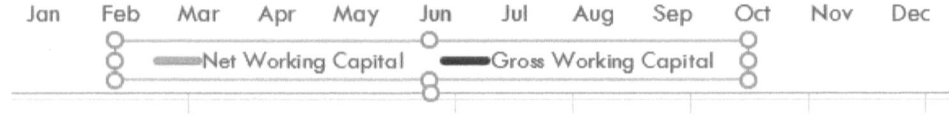

Jan   Feb   Mar   Apr   May   Jun   Jul   Aug   Sep   Oct   Nov   Dec

Net Working Capital   Gross Working Capital

13- Go to **Format** tab, **Shape Outline**, and click on **No Outline**.

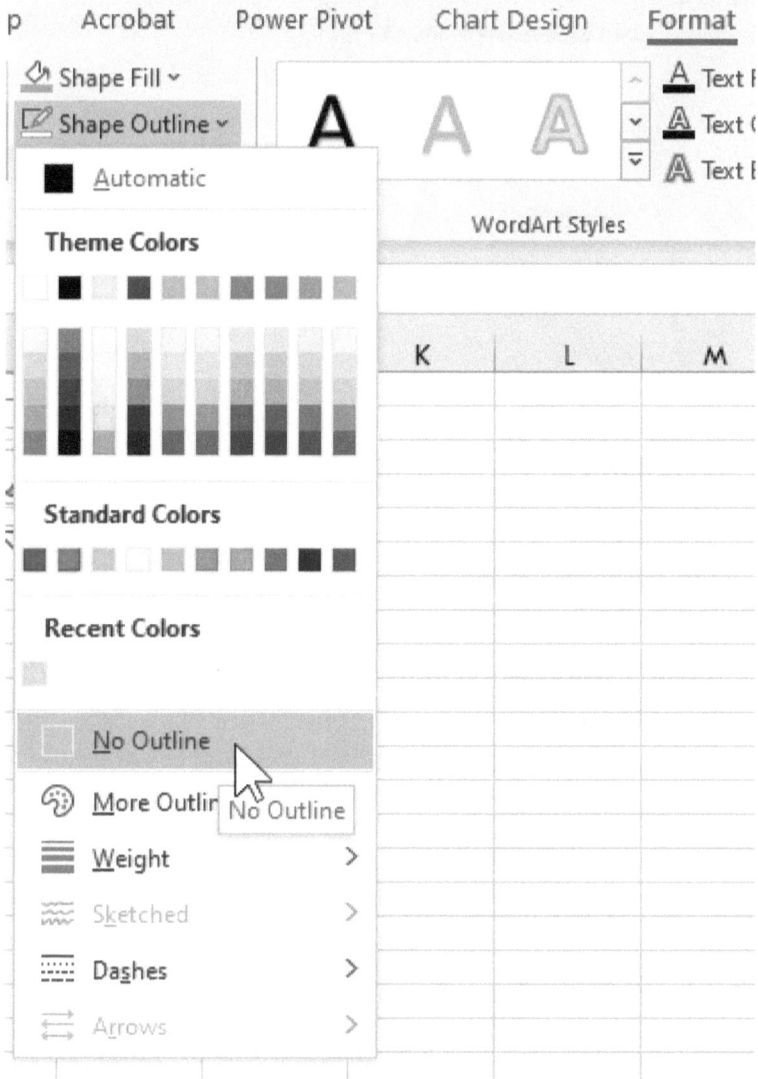

14- Right-click the **Chart Area** and click on **Move Chart.**

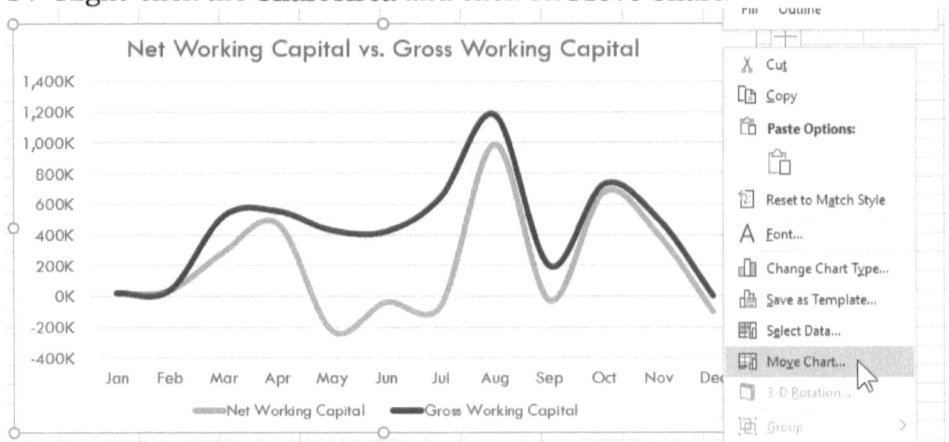

15- Check the option **Object in**, select **Dashboard**, and click OK.

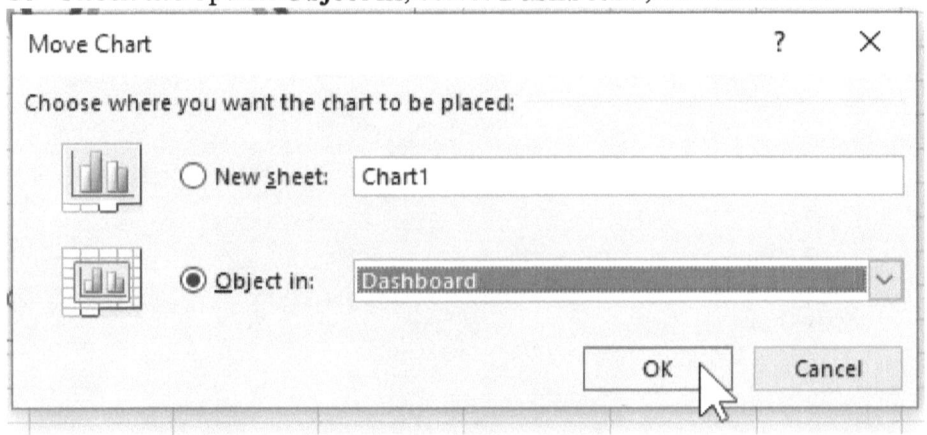

16- Select the chart, go to **Format** tab and change the **Height** to 10.93 cm, and the **Width** to 19.08 cm.

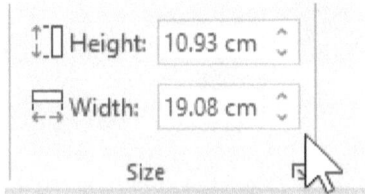

17- Drag and drop the objects to have a Dashboard like the image below.

11. Positive and Negative Numbers with Column Charts

1- Go to **Profit and Loss Summary** sheet.

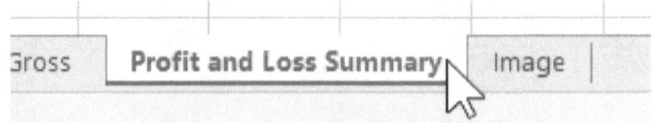

2- Select the range **A1:B13**. Then, go to **Insert** tab, **Charts** and select the **Clustered Column** chart.

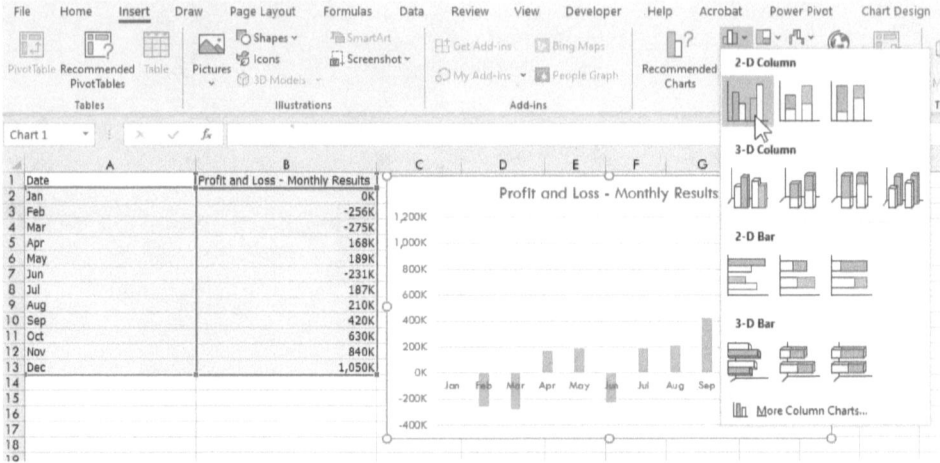

3- With the chart selected click on **Chart Elements** ("+" icon). Then, uncheck **Gridlines**.

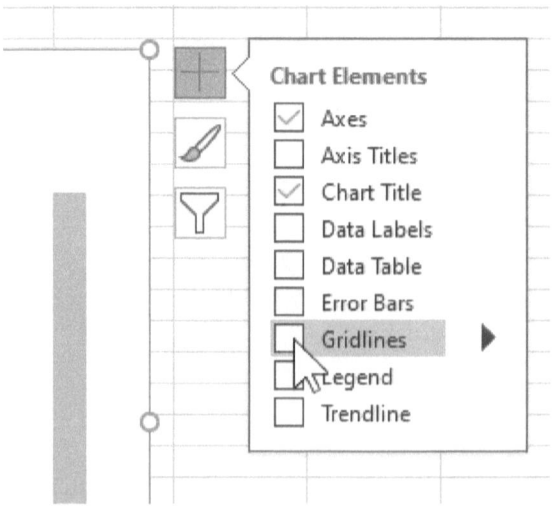

4- Go to **Axes** and uncheck **Primary Vertical**.

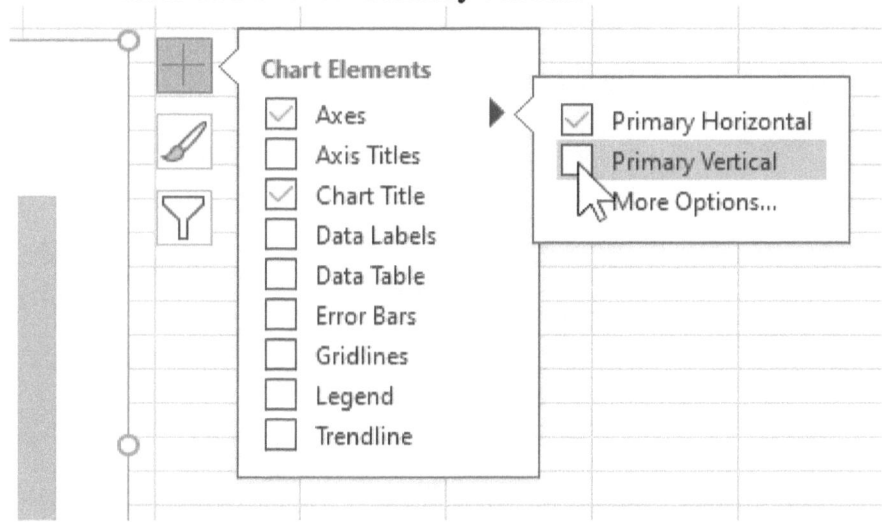

5- Right-click the any bar and click on **Format Data Series**.

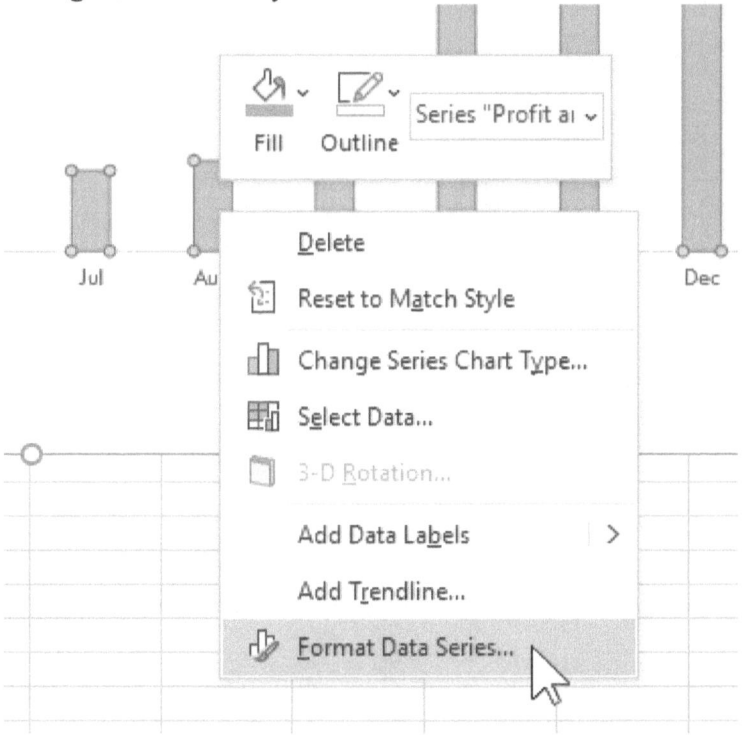

6- Go to **Fill** and select **Solid** fill. Then, check the option **Invert if negative.**

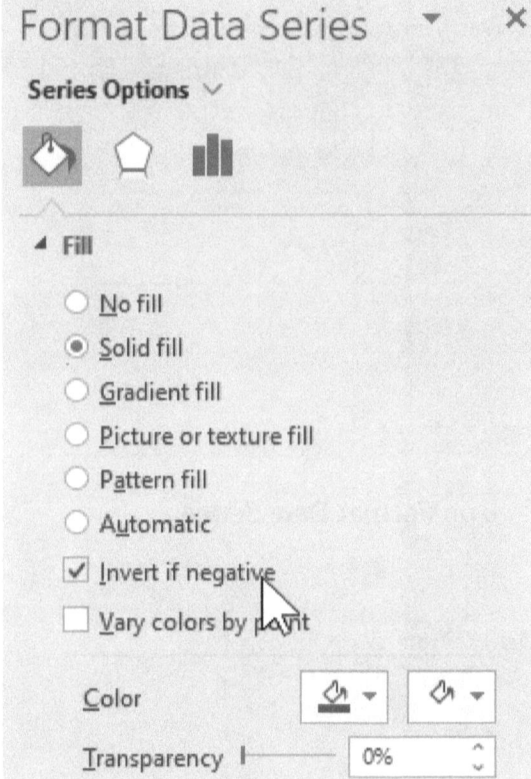

7- Change the **Fill color** to **Sky Blue, Background 2, Darker 50%**

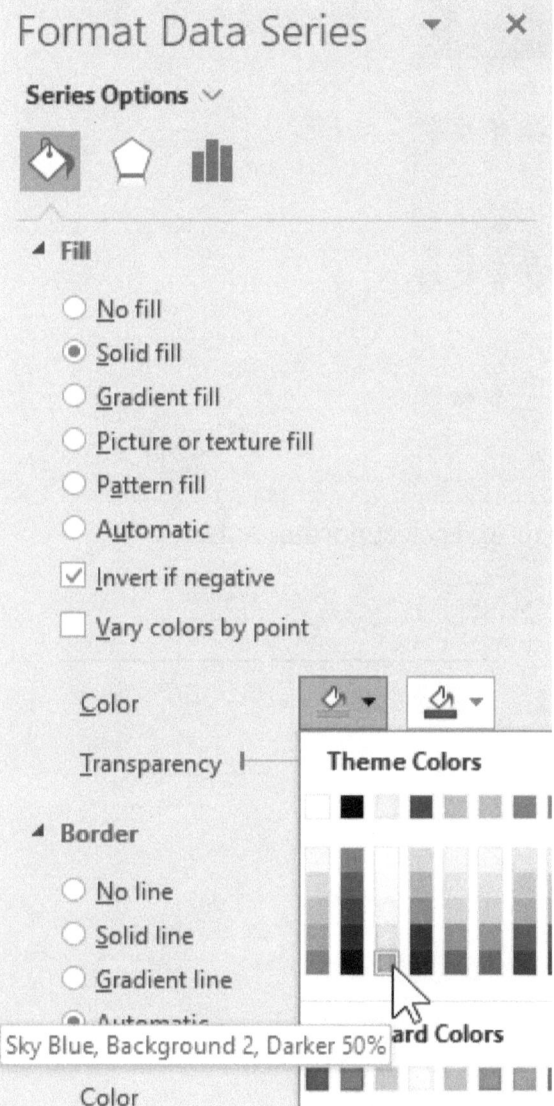

8- Change the **Inverted Fill color** to **Red, Accent 3, Darker 25%**

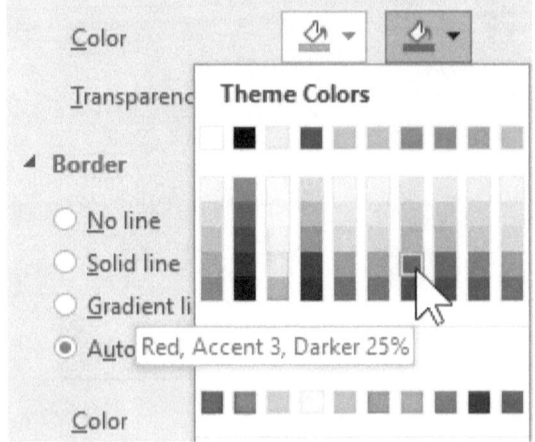

9- Right-click the horizontal axis and select **Format Axis**.

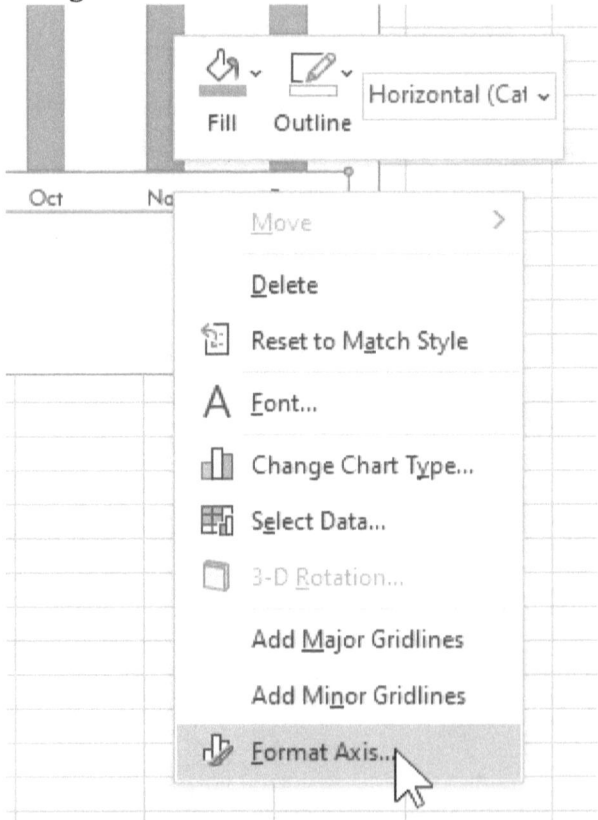

10- On **Axis Options** change the **Label Position** to **Low**.

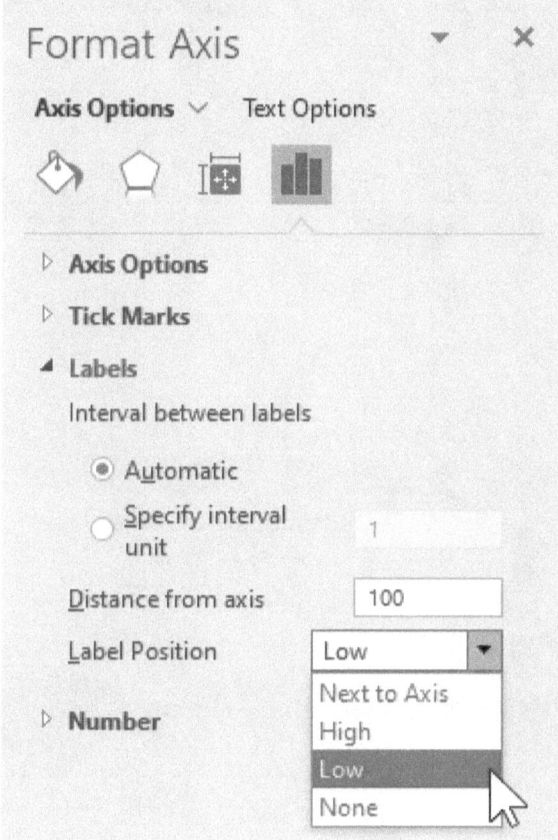

11- With the horizontal axis selected, change the **font size** to 12.

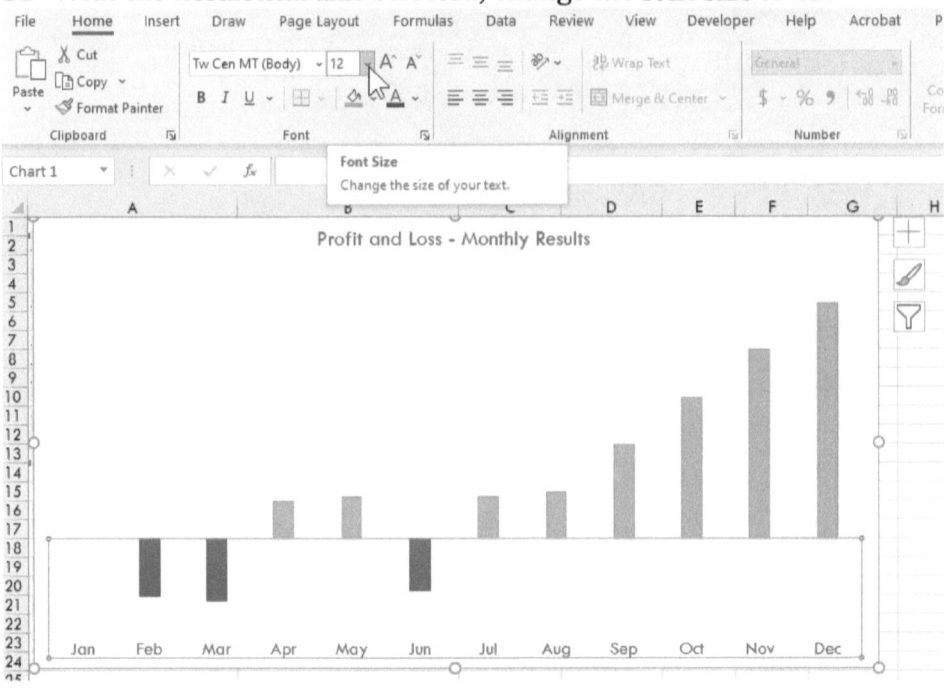

12- With the chart selected click on **Chart Elements** ("+" icon). Then, check **Data Labels**.

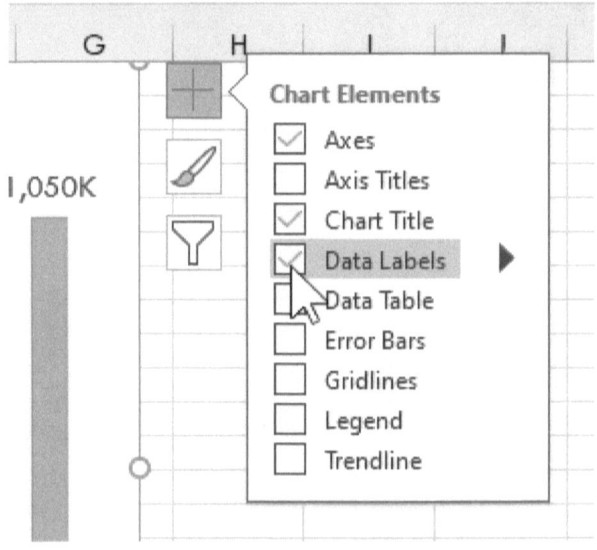

13- Right-click the **chart area** and select **Format Chart Area**.

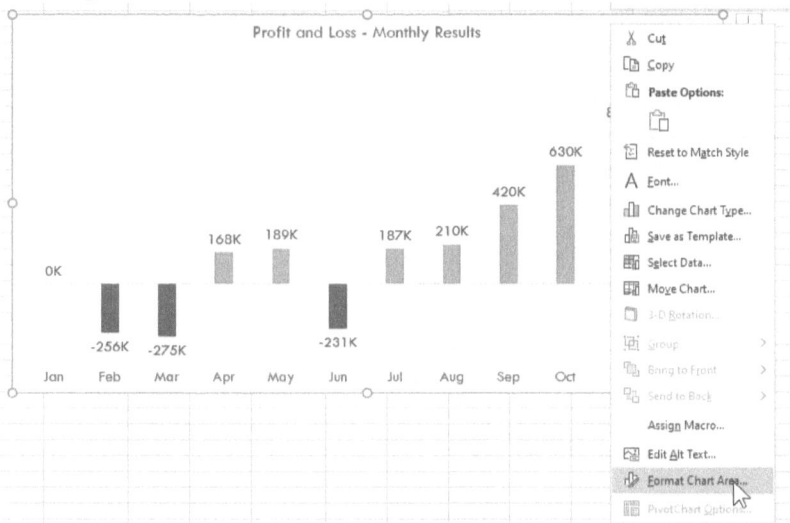

14- Check the option **Solid Fill** and change the color to **Dark Blue, Text 2, Darker 25%.**

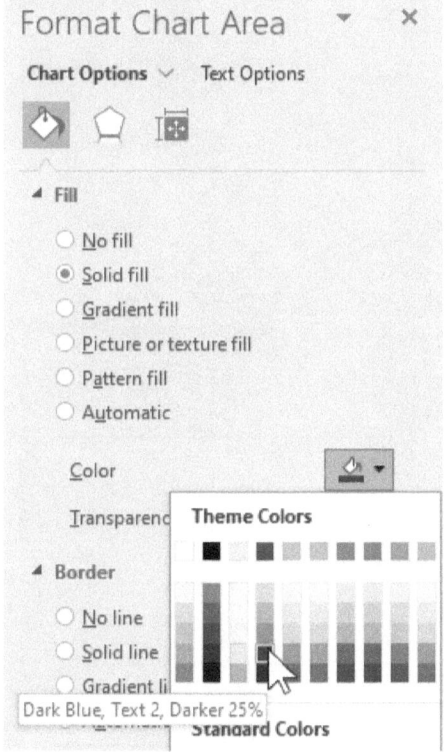

15- Go to **Text Options** tab. Then, go to **Text Fill** and check the option **Solid fill**. Change the **Color** to **White, Background 1**.

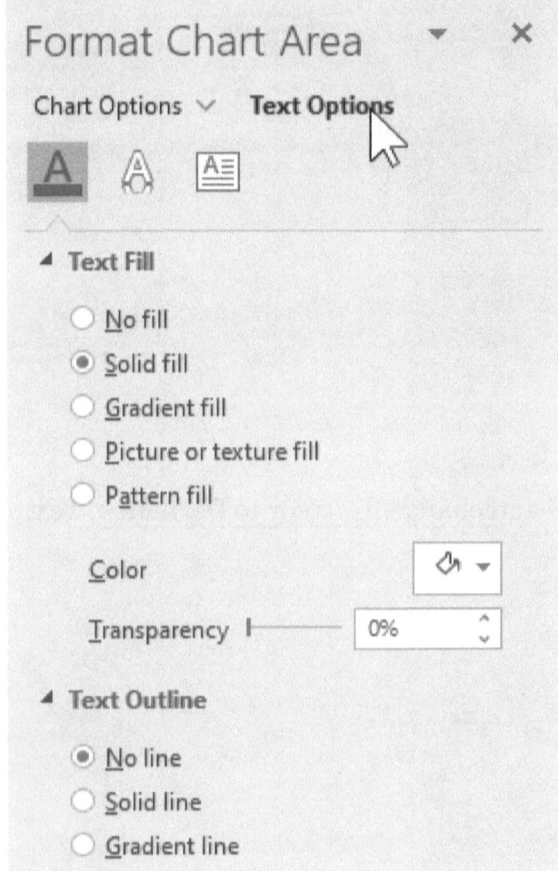

16- Right-click the **Chart Area** and click on **Move Chart**.

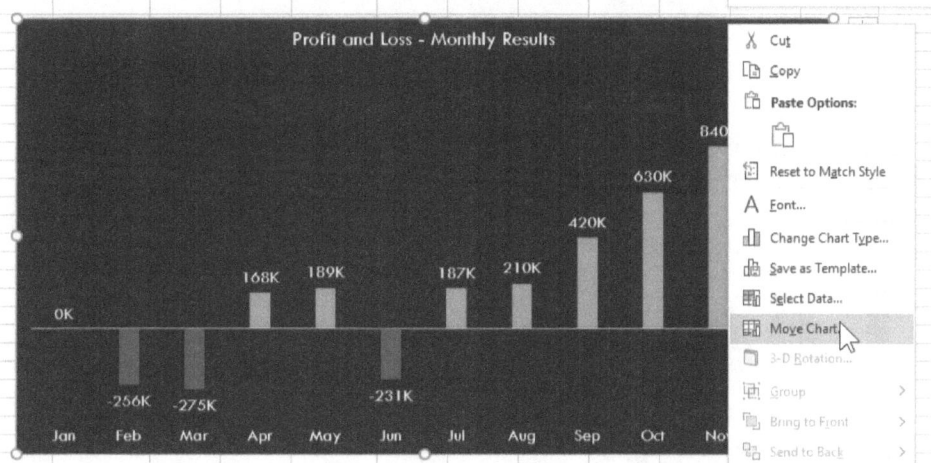

17- Check the option **Object in**, select **Dashboard**, and click OK.

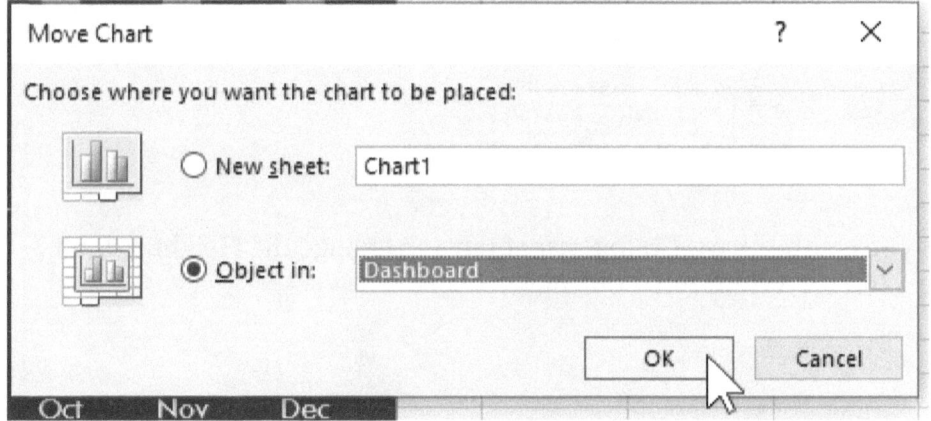

18- Go to **Format** tab, **Shape Outline**, and click on **No Outline**.

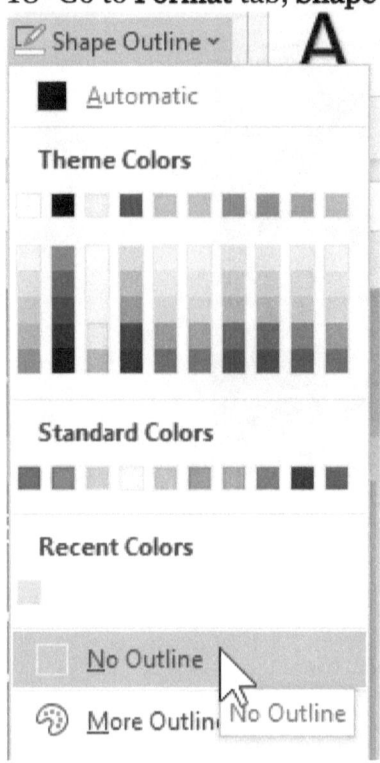

19- Select the chart. Go to **Format** tab and change the **Height** to 9.63 cm, and the **Width** to 19.08 cm.

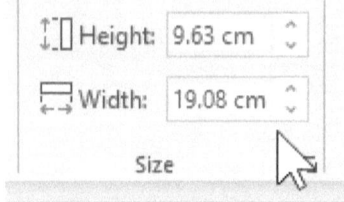

20- Drag and drop the objects to have a Dashboard like the image below.

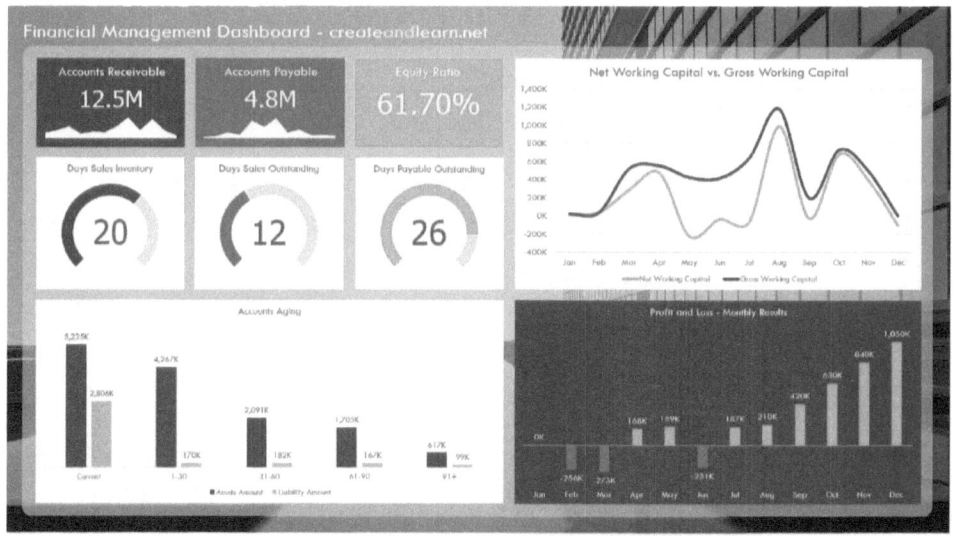

21- Use the **Align** tool when necessary.

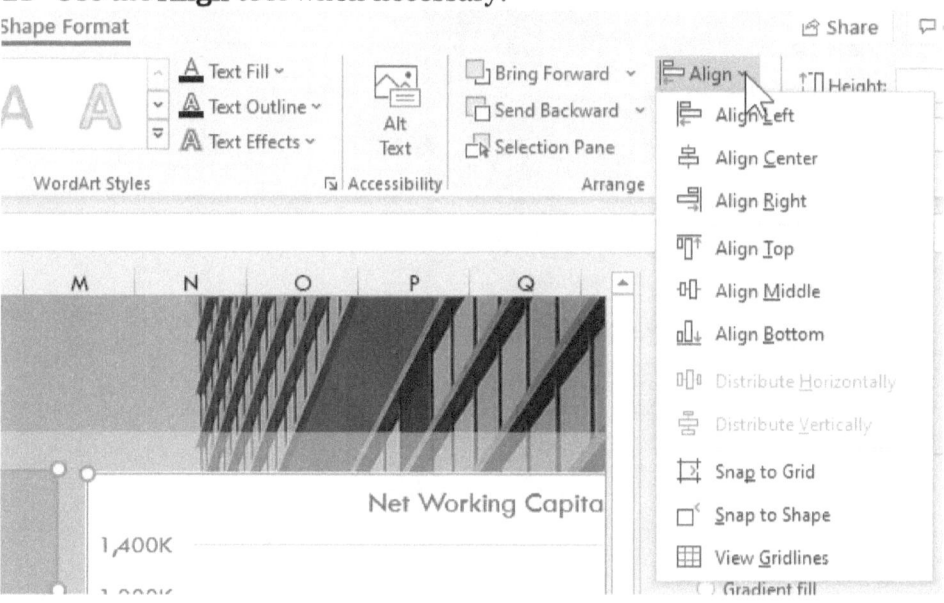

12.Presenting your Dashboard

Below you will find some useful tools to improve your Dashboard presentation, they aim to produce a cleaner view and are useful in meetings, presentations, and sharing.

Cleaning the Worksheet

Go to **Page Layout** tab and uncheck **Heading** and **Gridlines.**

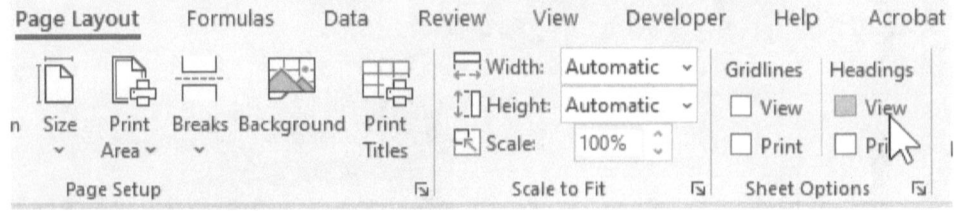

Hiding the Ribbon

Click on the **Ribbon display options** at the top-right of the window. Then, select **Auto-hide Ribbon**.

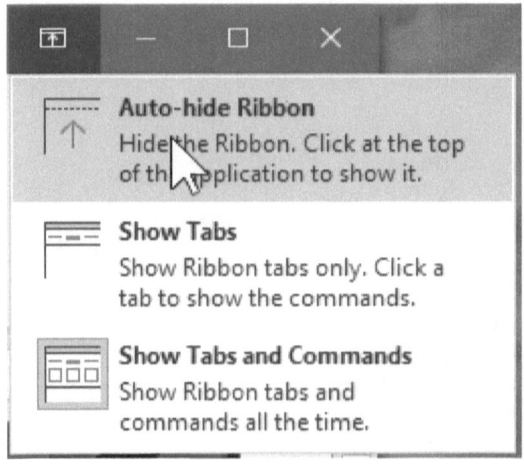

Click on **Show Tabs and Commands** to return to the previous way.

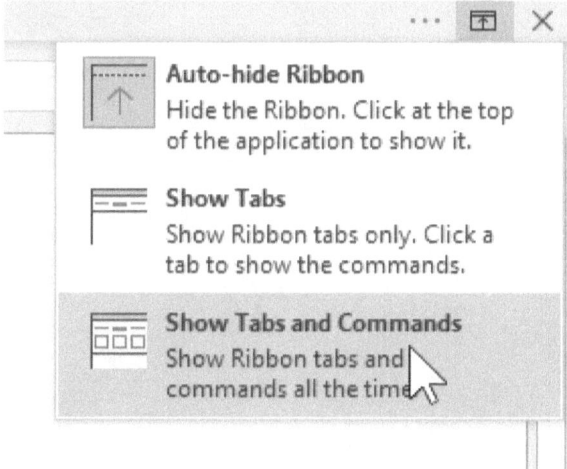

Page Break

If you need to change the printing area you can go to the **Page Break Preview**

Use the **blue border** to set the printing limits.

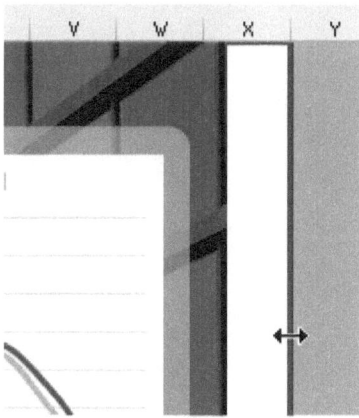

Click on **Normal** to return to the normal view.

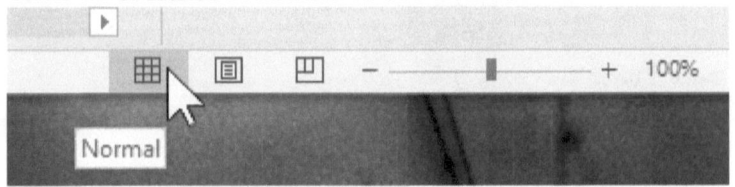

Page Setup

Go to **Page Layout** tab and click on **Page Setup**.

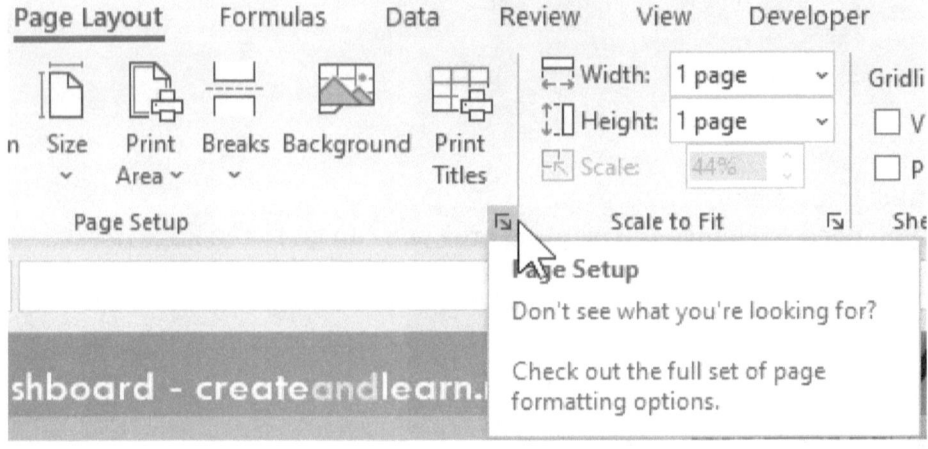

On **Page** tab, select **Landscape** and change the scaling to **Fit to: 1 page wide by 1 tall**.

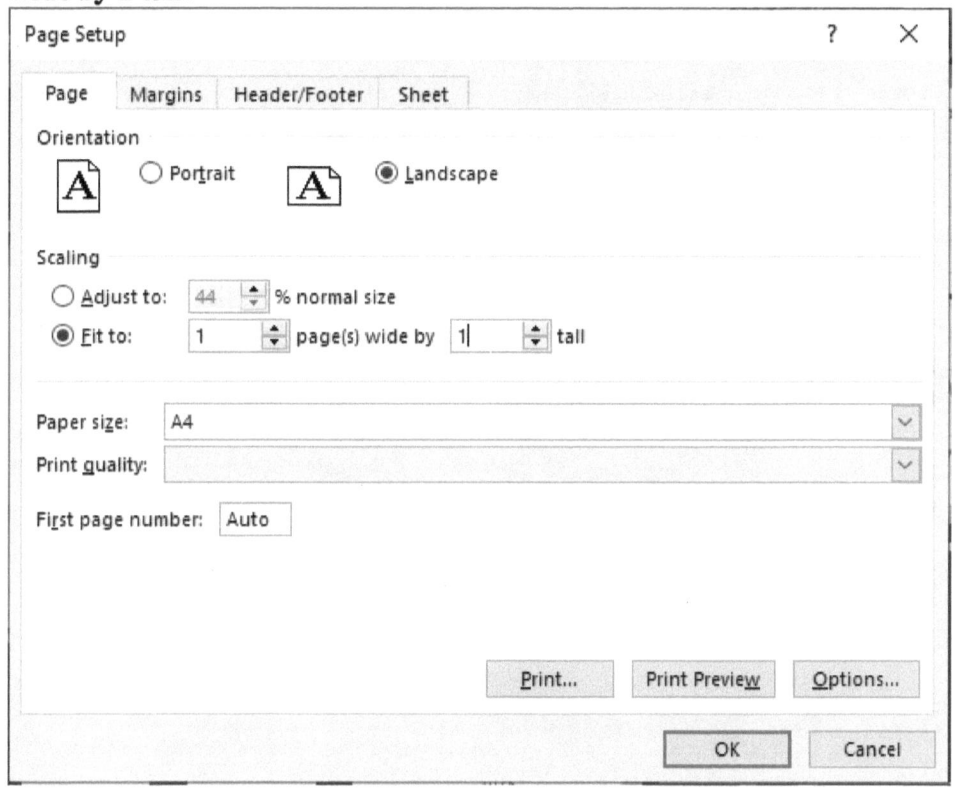

Go to **Margins** tab and check the options Center on page **Horizontally** and **Vertically.** Then, click on **Print Preview.**

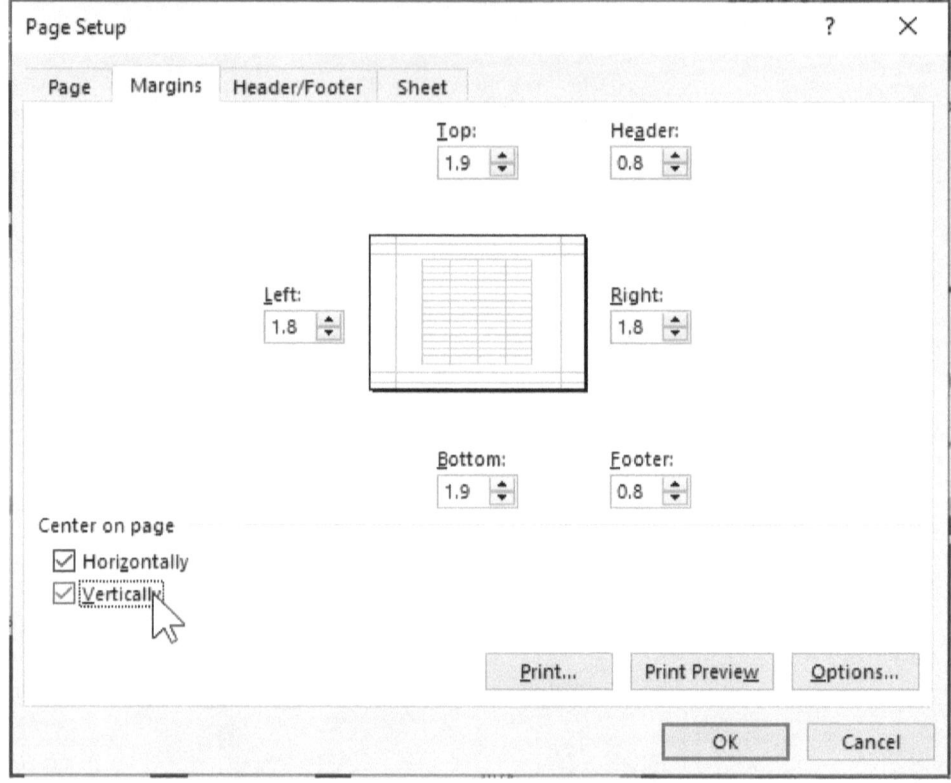

Microsoft Excel will display the printing area.

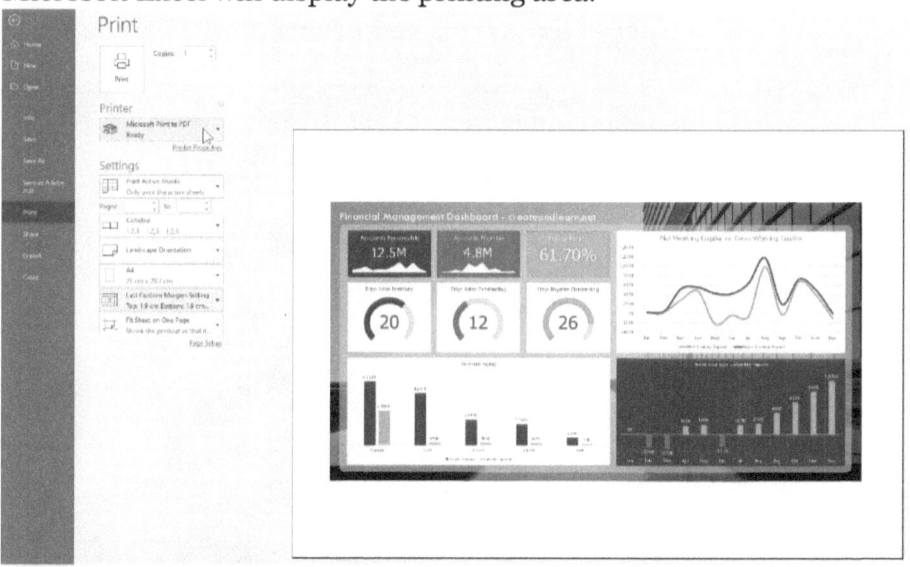

Click on **Back** to return to the dashboard.

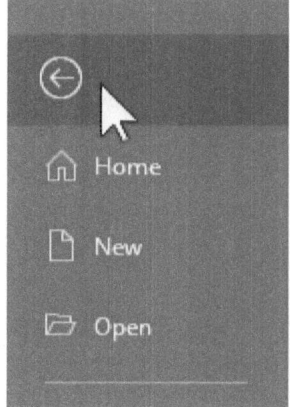

Congratulations! You have created a complete Dashboard using basic, intermediate, and advanced Excel tools and Dashboard Designing methods.

13. Dashboard Challenge

The Dashboard Challenge is a simple way to help you evolving on your dashboard skill. Below you will find the dashboard that you should try to replicate, and some tips to help you reaching the outcome.

Dashboard:

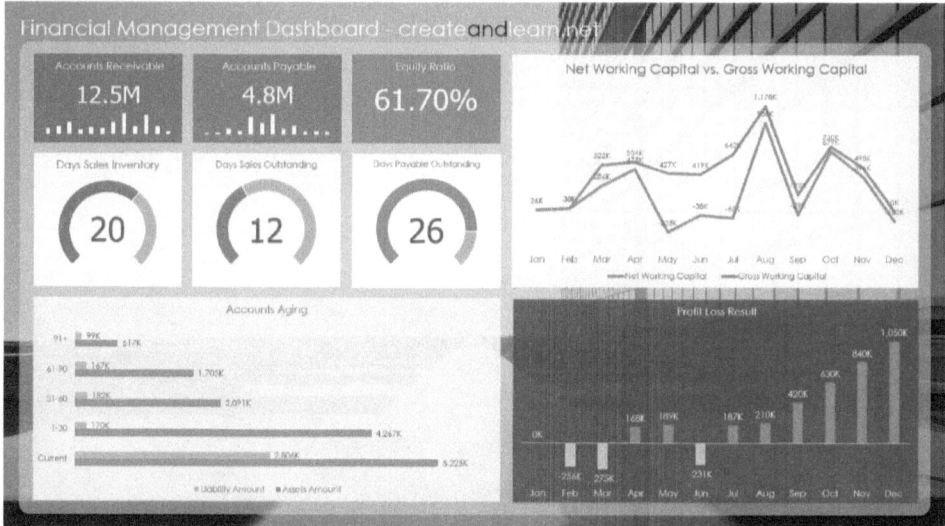

Tips:

1- The theme used in this dashboard was the **Savon**.

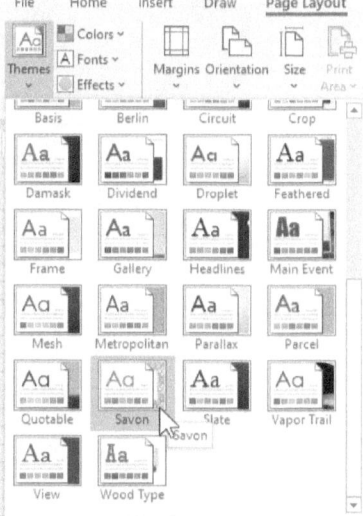

2- The chart used at the top was the **Clustered Column**.

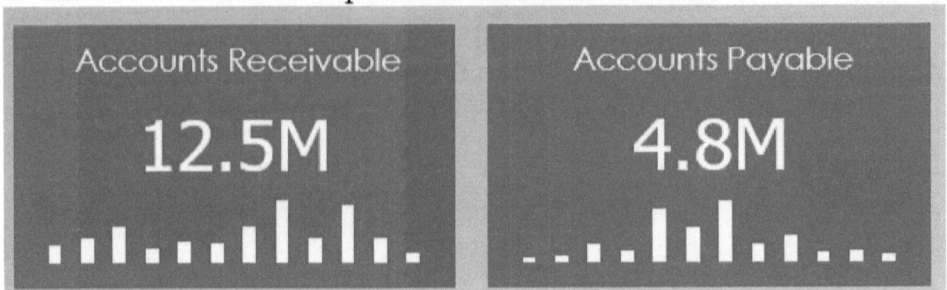

3- The chart used for the Accounts Aging was the **Clustered Bar**.

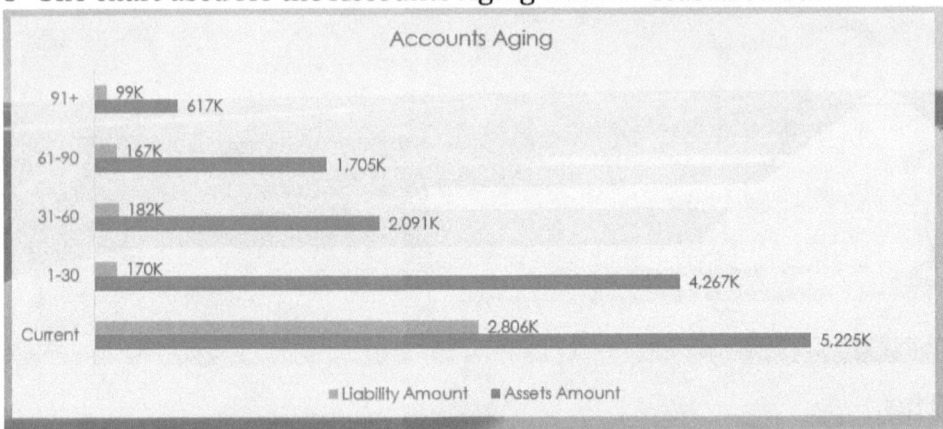

4- The chart area fill has a color transparency of 10%.

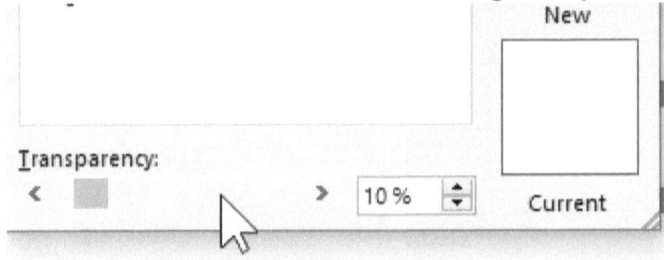

14.Next Steps

1- This book was created to help you to learn by doing and through practice, and to expand your knowledge in creating dashboard using Microsoft Excel.

If you want to keep practicing and improving your Dashboard skills through several industries, I have few recommendations:

1- Modify the current dashboard. Try using other types of graphics, fonts, themes, and visual.

2- Try to build the dashboard for this book without assistance. Refer to this book only when necessary.

3- Try other books from the **Excel Easy** series at createandlearn.net/exceleasy

4- Try the **Excel Power Suite** book from the **Business Intelligence Clinic** series and learn how to work with Power Query, Data Model, and Power Pivot.

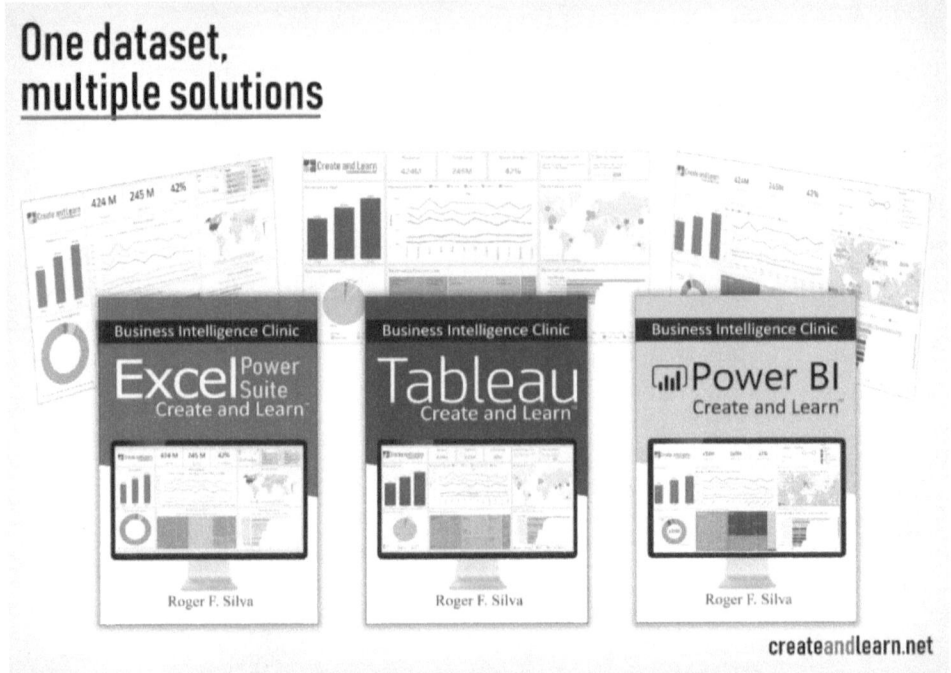

5- Ready to try something new? The **Power BI - Business Intelligence Clinic** is a great book to start learning Power BI, a fast-growing BI and data science tool.

Visit the page createandlearn.net to have access to these books and articles on data visualization.

6- Spread the word. Share your dashboard with colleagues and on social media like LinkedIn. Add me to your network so I can comment and check your progress.

7- Do not stop! Learning has never been more accessible. Search websites, books, videos, and keep studying. This is an excellent way to maintain a healthy brain and a promising career!

15. Final words

Thank you for the journey! We hope that you have enjoyed learning from this book as much as we have enjoyed writing and teaching the contents of this book.

What do you think of this book? We would like to ask you to take a minute to **review** this book. Reviews are incredibly important for our work.

If you have any comments or suggestions, please send us an e-mail or drop a message at our website — We would love to hear from you.

Thank you for the time we spent creating and learning.

Create and Learn team.

contact.createandlearn@gmail.com

createandlearn.net

You can find more Create and Learn books, files, articles, and videos:

https://www.createandlearn.net/

https://www.amazon.com/s?i=digital-text&rh=p_27%3ACreate+and+Learn

http://www.facebook.com/excelcreateandlearn

https://www.linkedin.com/company/create-and-learn

https://www.instagram.com/createandlearn_net/

https://www.youtube.com/channel/UCE4BQDcEuUE9lmCZfviSZLg/featured

For more **Create and Learn** books, visit
https://www.createandlearn.net/:

One dataset, multiple solutions

Business Intelligence Clinic — Excel Power Suite — Create and Learn — Roger F. Silva

Business Intelligence Clinic — Tableau — Create and Learn — Roger F. Silva

Business Intelligence Clinic — Power BI — Create and Learn — Roger F. Silva

createandlearn.net